101 STUNTS
FOR PRINCIPALS
TO INSPIRE STUDENT ACHIEVEMENT

For my Pop,
dispenser of Happy Grams and other positive reinforcements.

101 STUNTS
FOR PRINCIPALS
TO INSPIRE STUDENT ACHIEVEMENT

FRANK SENNETT

CORWIN PRESS
A Sage Publications Company
Thousand Oaks, California

For information:

Corwin Press
A Sage Publications Company
2455 Teller Road
Thousand Oaks, California 91320
www.corwinpress.com

Sage Publications Ltd.
1 Oliver's Yard
55 City Road
London EC1Y 1SP
United Kingdom

Sage Publications India Pvt. Ltd.
B-42, Panchsheel Enclave
Post Box 4109
New Delhi 110 017 India

Printed in the United States of America

Library of Congress Cataloging-in-Publication Data

Sennett, Frank.
101 stunts for principals to inspire student achievement / Frank Sennett.
    p. cm.
Includes bibliographical references and index.
ISBN 0-7619-8835-1 (cloth) — ISBN 0-7619-8836-X (pbk.)
    1. Motivation in education—United States-Humor. 2. School principals—United States—Humor. I. Title: One hundred one stunts for principals to inspire student achievement. II. Title: One hundred and one stunts for principals to inspire student achievement. III. Title.
LB1071.S46 2005
370.15′4—dc22   2004014431

This book is printed on acid-free paper.

03 04 05 06 10 9 8 7 6 5 4 3 2 1

Acquisitions Editor:	Elizabeth Brenkus
Editorial Assistant:	Candice Ling
Production Editor:	Diane S. Foster
Copy Editor:	Kristin Bergstad
Typesetter:	C&M Digitals (P) Ltd.
Proofreader:	Kathy Pollock
Graphic Designer:	Anthony Paular

Contents

Acknowledgments   xi

About the Author   xii

Introduction: Take the Motivational Stunt Challenge   xiii

1. Stunt Pros: Making the Case for Motivational Stunts   1

2. Set Up for Success: How to Lay
   the Groundwork for a Successful Motivational Stunt   4

3. Silly Suggestions, Boffo Blueprints,
   and Idiotic Ideas: 101 Stunts That Will
   Motivate Your Students to New Academic Heights   9

   No. 1. "The Razor's Edge." Have your
       head shaved during a special assembly   11

   No. 2. "Book the Bookmobile."
       Spend the day distributing books
       from the local public library's bookmobile   13

   No. 3. "Play Dead." Play the dead body
       during a *CSI*-style murder mystery event   15

   No. 4. "Cheer Up!" Become a school cheerleader for a day   17

   No. 5. "Robot Wars." Participate in
       a robotics unit that culminates in robot
       races or a gladiator-style demolition derby   18

   No. 6. "Bug Buffet." Make a meal of mealworms   20

   No. 7. "Mascot Mayhem." Dress up
       as your school's mascot for the day   23

   No. 8. "Clown Around." Show up at
       school decked out as a circus clown   24

   No. 9. "Marathon Plan." Promise to run a marathon
       if students meet a long-term educational goal   25

No. 10. "Hit the Roof." Move your office to the school roof — 27

No. 11. "Trading Places." Swap jobs
with a teacher, coach, or staff member for a day — 29

No. 12. "Crossed-Up Crossing Guard."
Direct traffic at school dressed in silly garb — 30

No. 13. "Pucker Up." Kiss a pig or other animal — 32

No. 14. "Human Sundae." Let students
dress you up as an ice-cream sundae — 34

No. 15. "Get In-Line." Strap on a pair
of skates and roll through the halls — 35

No. 16. "Karaoke Kings and
Queens." Sing along to your favorite hits — 36

No. 17. "Dance Fever." Host a backwards prom,
or "morp," and cut a rug in front of the student body — 37

No. 18. "Cross-Dressing Camp."
Dress up like a member of the opposite sex — 38

No. 19. "The Silent Treatment." Exercise your
right to remain silent for an entire school day — 40

No. 20. "Duct Tape Delights."
Allow students to duct-tape you to a wall — 41

No. 21. "Up, Up, and Away." Soar
over your school in a hot-air balloon — 42

No. 22. "Superheroic Stunts." Transform yourself
from mild-mannered educator into superhero for a day — 44

No. 23. "In the Swim."
Go jump in a lake—or even the ocean — 46

No. 24. "Saddle Up." Prance around
the school on the back of a horse or mule — 47

No. 25. "The Mysterious Reader."
Promote literacy with a "mystery reader"
program that brings in fascinating guest storytellers — 48

No. 26. "Dye Laughing." Get a crazy
dye job in front of the student body — 50

No. 27. "Bungee Banzai!" Hang out in front of the
school by your ankle after jumping off a bungee platform — 52

No. 28. "Slime Time." Let students
cover you in radioactive-green "slime" — 53

No. 29. "What a Character!" Dress up as a gorilla
or other goofy character and go ape in front of students — 55

No. 30. "Camping on Campus."
Set up a tent and host a sleepover at school — 57

No. 31. "The Condiment Caper." Dress up
like a hot dog in a cardboard or foam-rubber
bun, and allow students to add the fixings   58

No. 32. "Pie Fight!" Take a pie in
the face to reward student achievement   60

No. 33. "Everything's Backwards"
Declare a backwards day at school   61

No. 34. "Good Sports." Challenge a local college
or professional sports star to a one-on-one contest   62

No. 35. "Take a Tumble." Do a
somersault for each book students read   64

No. 36. "Eggcellent!" Lie down in a bed of rotten eggs   65

No. 37. "Got Milk?" Milk a cow at a special
school assembly   66

No. 38. "Where in the World?" Challenge students
to track you down at school as part of a geography unit   68

No. 39. "Cereal Thriller." Jump into a giant bowl of
milk while wearing a suit studded with Rice Krispies   69

No. 40. "Obstacle Coursing." Run the wackiest
obstacle course students can dream up   70

No. 41. "Disappearing Act." Enlist a local
magician to make you disappear into thin air   71

No. 42. "The Big Bucks." Ride a mechanical bull and
try to keep from getting bucked off in front of students   72

No. 43. "Hypnosis Hullabaloo." Bring in
a hypnotist to put you into a trance in front of students   73

No. 44. "Pie by the Pound."
Challenge students to a pie-eating contest   74

No. 45. "'Chute the Works." Go skydiving
to reward sky-high student achievement   75

No. 46. "Room-o-Sumo." Wrestle students,
faculty, and staff members in giant foam sumo suits   77

No. 47. "Puddles of Pudding."
Roll around in a pool of pudding   78

No. 48. "Snake Handling." Wrap
yourself in a boa—a boa constrictor, that is   80

No. 49. "Literary Theft." Portray a
favorite character from children's literature   81

No. 50. "Record Breaking." Help set a world record   83

No. 51. "Velcro Flight." Launch yourself
against a Velcro wall in a Velcro suit   85

No. 52. "Get Dunked." Let students
   try to dump you into a dunk tank   86

No. 53. "Waiting Around."
   Wait tables in the school cafeteria   88

No. 54. "Kid for a Day." Swap
   places with a student for a day   89

No. 55. "Dummy Up." Perform a
   ventriloquism routine for students   90

No. 56. "Check Mates."
   Participate in a game of human chess   91

No. 57. "Get the Point."
   Recline on a bed of nails   93

No. 58. "Treemendous!" Move
   your office into a tree for the day   94

No. 59. "Take a Dive." Jump off the high
   dive into a swimming pool fully clothed   95

No. 60. "Climbing the Wall." Scale a climbing
   wall to reward top-flight student achievements   96

No. 61. "Split Personality." Enlist
   a magician to saw you in half   97

No. 62. "Bake-Off!" Participate in a faculty
   and staff bake-off with student judges   98

No. 63. "Pigskin Classic." Chase down
   and attempt to catch a greased pig   99

No. 64. "Monkey Business." Bring
   in a monkey to do your job for a day   100

No. 65. "Rock On!" Perform in a faculty-staff rock band   100

No. 66. "Reading Marathon." Read
   stories aloud for an entire school day   101

No. 67. "All Wet." Subject
   yourself to a barrage of water balloons   103

No. 68. "Just One Hitch." Get married at school   104

No. 69. "Bound for Success." Let students
   tie you to a cafeteria chair during lunch hour   105

No. 70. "Stage Fright."
   Play a cameo role in the school play   106

No. 71. "Balancing the Books."
   Compete in a book-balancing contest   107

No. 72. "Step Into the Ring."
   Participate in a mock pro wrestling match   108

No. 73. "A Real Goal Getter." Play
   soccer or floor hockey goalie and give
   every child a free shot from the penalty line   109

No. 74. "Seuss for Breakfast." Serve
    students a breakfast of green eggs and ham   109
No. 75. "A Change in the Weather."
    Fill in for a local TV weatherman   111
No. 76. "Bubbly Performance." Step into
    a tank of water while wearing an Alka-Seltzer suit   112
No. 77. "Rube the Day." Challenge
    students to build a giant Rube Goldberg
    device that does something wacky to you   113
No. 78. "Three-Wheelin'." Participate in a tricycle race   114
No. 79. "Construction Fun."
    Spend the day high above your
    school in a construction cherry picker   115
No. 80. "Bee Bearded." Wear a beard of bees   116
No. 81. "Harness Your Energy." Pull children
    around the school grounds in a horse cart   117
No. 82. "Bus Road-e-o." Drive a school bus
    through a parking-lot obstacle course   118
No. 83. "Hang Around, Around the Clock."
    Spend 24 straight hours at school   119
No. 84. "Dodge City." Compete in an adults
    versus children dodge ball tournament   120
No. 85. "Slip 'n' Sliding Away." Launch
    yourself down a Slip 'n' Slide on the school lawn   121
No. 86. "Have a Field Day." Pit the faculty and
    staff against students in a schoolwide Olympiad   122
No. 87. "Sleep With the Fishes."
    Step into a vat filled with live fish   123
No. 88. "School Idol." Hold
    an *American Idol*-style singing contest   124
No. 89. "Frozen Moments."
    Spend the day appearing at various
    places around the school frozen like a statue   125
No. 90. "Hit Parade." Get silly on a parade float   125
No. 91. "Gym Dandy."
    Perform a wild gymnastics routine   126
No. 92. "Later 'Gator." Wrestle an alligator   127
No. 93. "Punkin' Chunkin'."
    Participate in a "punkin' chunkin'" contest   128
No. 94. "April Foolishness." Get silly on April Fool's Day   129
No. 95. "Pole Vaulting." Sit atop a flagpole for the day   132
No. 96. "Eat Your Hat." Eat a baked facsimile
    of a hat when students attain a difficult academic goal   133

No. 97. "Stupid Human Trickery."
   Participate in a Stupid Human Tricks
   assembly showcasing the silly hidden
   talents of teachers, administrators, and even parents   134
No. 98. "Weird Science Fair."
   Illustrate fascinating scientific
   phenomena through a series of silly experiments   135
No. 99. "Color Coding." Adopt
   a color-based theme for the day   136
No. 100. "Fear Factor Assembly." Face your
   phobias and participate in a series of gross activities   138
No. 101. "Luck of the Draw." Allow students to select
   the stunt you'll perform if they reach an academic goal   139

4. **Don't Try This at School:**
   How to Avoid a Stunt Gone Wrong   141

5. **Alert the Media: How to**
   Generate Positive Press for Your Stunt   144

References   147

Acknowledgments

I was inspired to write this book by the many educators who employ motivational stunts to make school more fun for students and encourage their academic explorations. In particular, I wish to thank Alan Cook, who shared many wonderful insights into crafting a stunt that can be linked to the entire curriculum.

I tip my silly hat to the fine professionals at Corwin for bringing this book out. I'm also grateful to my family for their support. Thanks especially to my wife, Heather, for watching the new little guy while dad finished his writing.

Corwin Press gratefully acknowledges the contributions of the following individuals:

Bill Cecil
Cofounder, Best Year Ever!®
'03-'04 Michigan Teacher of the Year
Mason, MI

Kevin Fillgrove
Principal
Hershey Middle School
Hershey, PA

Deborah Friant
Principal
Monroe Elementary School
Norman, OK

Jan Griffin
Assistant Principal
Ocean Springs Middle School
Ocean Springs, MS

J. Victor McGuire
Instructor
College of Education
University of Nevada
Las Vegas, NV

Gerald Tirozzi
Executive Director
National Association of Secondary School Principals (NASSP)

Caryl Thomason
Superintendent
Cheyenne Mountain District 12
Colorado Springs, CO

Bonnie Tryon
'02-'03 NAESP Board of Directors
Principal
Golding Elementary School
Cobleskill, NY

Paul Young
'02-'03 NAESP Board of Directors
Principal, Corwin Author
West Elementary School
Lancaster, OH

About the Author

 **Frank Sennett** earned his fiction MFA from the University of Montana, and now teaches creative writing for UCLA Extension. He has served as editor of the K–12 journal *Curriculum Review* for nearly a decade. His first book from Corwin Press was 2004's *400 Quotable Quotes From the World's Leading Educators.* To book Frank for a seminar on motivational stunts, please contact the Corwin Press Speakers' Bureau. Call (800) 818–7243, and press 5.

Introduction

Take the Motivational Stunt Challenge

As a dedicated educator, review the following school-improvement wish list and dare to dream. Are you:

- Searching for a sure-fire method of motivating students to great academic heights and sky-high standardized test scores? *It's up on the school roof.*
- Trying to create a closer-knit educational community? *Dress (up) for success.*
- Looking to leapfrog past your fundraising goals? *The answer's staring you right in the kisser.*
- Hoping to make a positive splash with local reporters? *It's only a wading-pool dive away.*
- Itching to weave together cross-curricular units with style? *Challenge students to give you a hair-razing experience.*
- Feeling pressured to do all of the above—without devouring your budget? *There's a tasty solution waiting inside a whipped-cream pie.*

Whether you're an administrator, teacher, counselor, or school librarian, performing a motivational stunt can help you meet every one of the goals above in a fun and creative way that students—and their parents—will remember fondly for years. All it takes is a smidgen of creativity, a dollop of elbow grease, and the willingness to poke a bit of good-natured fun at yourself.

PLAYING THE "GOTCHA" GAME

"For kids, getting the teacher or, ultimately, the principal is the best thing you can do," contends Alan Cook, a California grade school principal who inspires his students to meet impressive reading goals with a new stunt challenge every year.

Among his many daring feats, Cook has eaten bugs, sprawled on a mound of rotten eggs, and spent the day atop a 60-foot construction cherry picker to reward the academic achievements of his students.

"School is serious, but that doesn't mean they're not kids and they don't enjoy having a good time while they're here," Cook says. "We make the stunt the theme for the whole year. When I lay down on eggs, one of our fifth-grade classes figured out how many eggs it would take to fill a certain size container. When I promised to eat bugs if they met a reading goal, the kids from first grade on were writing bug recipes, we had entomologists in to talk about different bugs and their habitats, and so on. We use stunts as a learning tool."

HOW FAR WILL YOU GO
TO HELP STUDENTS GO FAR?

One of the great things about performing a motivational stunt is that you can tailor it to your own personality and comfort level. If you're not quite up for swimming in a pool full of pudding, for instance, you might be willing to read the morning announcements over a bullhorn from the school roof. Or if a meal of mealworms proves too repulsive, dyeing your hair green for a day may prove a more palatable alternative.

Whichever stunt feels right for you, if you couple it with a creative educational challenge and incorporate the theme throughout the curriculum, your students will be laughing all the way to the knowledge bank by the time you take the stage.

Ready to set up a winning motivational stunt of your own? The following chapters will take you through the entire process step by step, from finding a fun idea and enlisting the support of the community to setting a challenging goal and getting positive press for creatively boosting the academic achievement of your students.

Use the wealth of stunt suggestions, cross-curricular project tie-in tips, and case studies of master motivators to become the newest member of the motivational stunt hall of fame. And whatever else you do, have fun with the process. After all, this is one endeavor in which playing the fool can generate serious rewards for your students and school community.

1 Stunt Pros

Making the Case for Motivational Stunts

Child psychologists and educational researchers suggest that performing an occasional silly stunt to spur academic achievement is a healthy way for teachers and administrators to have fun with their role as authority figures. Displaying a sense of humor won't undermine the respect students have for instructors and principals. But it will help kids see them as well-rounded human beings.

A motivational stunt "works because it's something odd," says Texas psychologist Jerald Gottlieb (Gillman, 2000). "It shows kids that something is possible that they thought was impossible. You've just introduced something that's an exception to the rule." And it's an exception that can inspire exceptional educational achievement.

Mark Baldwin, an education professor at California State University-San Marcos, further suggests that educators who perform stunts are "showing some connection, support" for their students (Jenkins, 2000). "They want kids to know they're with them." And children tend to respond academically when they believe their teachers and administrators are taking a positive, personal interest in their education.

STELLAR STUNTS, AMAZING RESULTS

So motivational stunts can be fun, inexpensive exercises in community building. But do these challenges really deliver the educational goods? A growing number of administrators and teachers offer solid—and smile-inducing—proof that they do.

- Janis Stonebreaker, principal of Ottoman Elementary in Orangevale, California, dressed up as a princess, kissed a frog, and belted out "Someday My Prince Will Come" after her 400 students shattered their goal of reading for 500,000 minutes in six months by nearly 20,000 minutes.
- Mark Soss, principal of Roaring Brook Elementary in Chappaqua, New York, shaved off the beard he'd worn for 30 years after his 650 students kept a pledge to give up TV for reading and other activities.
- Janet Franklin, principal of Beaumont Elementary in Knoxville, Tennessee, turned herself into a hot dog complete with cardboard "bun" and encouraged students who exceeded a coupon-book sales goal to decorate her costume with ketchup, relish, and other messy condiments.
- Ron Hanson, a teacher at Fisher Primary School in Bellingham, Washington, exchanged pies in the face with principal Brad Jernberg after students read on their own time for at least 20 minutes every day for a month. The assembly performance also celebrated the school's first-place finish in a state science competition.
- Alex Bacos, a counselor at Madison Middle School in North Hollywood, California, dressed up as the Little Mermaid—complete with seashell halter-top and gold sequined skirt. He warbled songs from the Disney film after students raised their collective score on the state's Stanford 9 test by an impressive 66 points.

CRITICAL OF STUNTS? LIGHTEN UP

In recent years, an increasing number of researchers have called into question the propriety and long-term efficacy of employing behaviorist motivational techniques in the classroom. It was claimed that in addition to disempowering their subjects (Kohn, 1993), these techniques can decrease children's intrinsic motivation to learn (Deci, Ryan, & Koestner, 1999). I agree with many criticisms of human behaviorism in general (it tends to devolve into a dehumanizing power trip for practitioners), and motivational rewards in particular (they're unnecessary because, as the engaging Alfie Kohn puts it in *Punished by Rewards*, "we are beings who possess natural curiosity about ourselves and our environment, who search for and overcome challenges, who try to master skills and attain competence, and who seek to reach new levels of complexity in what we learn and do").

But motivational stunts belong in a different, far healthier class of rewards than stickers, pizzas, or cash, for a couple of reasons. First of all, these stunts shine a spotlight on how much fun learning can be while celebrating collective accomplishments. Second, they offer students no tangible reward in exchange for increased effort or achievement. Instead, the stunts merely show children the human side of their school administrators. They reveal educators taking such a personal interest in students that they are willing to act silly to encourage academic success. In essence, then, motivational stunts are an "empowering trip" for students, not a power trip for educators. These all-hands activities bring school communities closer together, and they inject a sense of play into the educational process even as they encourage higher achievement.

Other critics are more offended by the silly aspects of motivational stunts than they are by the idea of offering rewards for achievement. As one principal put it, "I just wonder whether the humanistic approach to the profession doesn't cause us to lose the professionalism that we'd all like to have, the respect that all educators keep saying we don't get. If we don't act like professionals, how can we expect to be treated like professionals?" (Fetbrandt, 1996). But it becomes necessary to reject the notion that educators should adopt the buttoned-down demeanor common in many other disciplines when one considers a key ingredient those professions lack: a total focus on children. Creating a vibrant school community and delivering strong educational results should be enough to engender respect for any teacher or administrator—even if he or she spends one day a year engaging students through childlike play.

Set Up for Success

How to Lay the Groundwork for a Successful Motivational Stunt

Take the following simple steps before performing your stunt to avoid getting figurative egg on your face even as you take a real pie in the kisser.

1. Select an appropriate stunt. The 101 stunts outlined in Chapter 3 are rated on both silliness level and gross-out potential to help you pick one you'll be comfortable performing. Other questions to ask yourself during the selection process: Will students be excited to see me attempt this stunt? Can I link it to the school's most important academic goals? Will it enjoy the approval of the greater school community, including parents, board members, and the local media? Do I have the resources on hand to pull off the stunt—or can I easily generate funds and in-kind contributions to underwrite it?

2. Enlist the support of the school community. Secure faculty and PTA buy-in before announcing the stunt. Solicit their ideas and ask them to help you pull it off. Consider giving them three or four stunt choices to select from so they feel some ownership of the initiative. Discuss the plan with your superintendent, providing the clear value proposition that successful stunts boost student achievement, raise school morale, and generate positive press coverage for little or no cost. Support your arguments with examples from the book.

Veteran motivational stunt performers stress the importance of involving the entire school community in the process. Explains Principal Alan Cook, who performs a different stunt every year for the high-achieving students of Orangevale, California's Green Oaks Fundamental Elementary, "Parents and other people make suggestions and I have a parent liaison who's a master at helping me put these things together. Most of the ideas come from her." Adds Cook, "We brainstorm now for about two weeks before announcing the stunt, and try to think of all the negatives." Before he reclined into a container full of rotten eggs, for instance, "One of my concerns was that people would perceive that we were wasting food, so we made sure to call farms and stores and find out that they would actually toss these normally anyway. Get input from parents and teachers so you know all of the downsides."

Six Popular Motivational Stunt Goals

1. Reading a certain number of books or pages.

2. Boosting standardized test scores by a certain percentage.

3. Completing a schoolwide service-learning project.

4. Increasing participation in designated afterschool programs by a targeted amount.

5. Involving a set percentage of parents in the local PTA or PTO.

6. Bringing in a targeted amount of money through a fundraising drive.

---

3. Adopt an ambitious schoolwide achievement goal. Most motivational stunts are tied into reading goals. Principals promise to perform the stunts if the students collectively read a certain number of books or pages during a designated period ranging from a month to a full school year. But stunts easily can be linked to increases in standardized test scores instead. In fact, anything students can do collectively can be pegged to a motivational stunt. Other examples include participation in afterschool programs, completion of service-learning projects, and even conducting successful fundraising drives. Enlist parent volunteers, faculty, and staff members on a stunt steering committee that will help you adopt a meaningful goal. In parent communications, never mention the stunt without also discussing the specific student achievement it's promoting.

Stunts That Connect to Specific Educational Goals

Most stunts outlined in this book can be tied into just about any schoolwide achievement goal. But several of the activities match up particularly well with one aspect of the curriculum. Here's a cheat sheet of the most subject-specific stunts:

Reading

No. 2: Book the Bookmobile

No. 25: The Mysterious Reader

No. 49: Literary Theft

No. 66: Reading Marathon

No. 71: Balancing the Books

No. 74: Seuss for Breakfast

Science & Math

No. 3: Play Dead

No. 5: Robot Wars

No. 21: Up, Up and Away

No. 22: Superheroic Stunts

No. 45: 'Chute the Works

No. 75: A Change in the Weather

No. 77: Rube the Day

No. 93: Punkin' Chunkin'

No. 98: Weird Science Fair

Health & Fitness

No. 9: Marathon Plan

No. 23: In the Swim

No. 35: Take a Tumble

No. 73: A Real Goal Getter

No. 86: Have a Field Day

No. 91: Gym Dandy

Social Studies

No. 38: Where in the World?

4. Make the stunt the centerpiece of a yearlong theme. Start by brainstorming a fun slogan linked to the stunt, and then work with teachers to develop activities across the curriculum that tie into the theme. For instance, if you've agreed to let a magician saw you in half when students meet an important academic goal, you could adopt a "Learning Is Magic" theme and encourage teachers to link as many activities as possible to magic.

It's fun and easy to relate your curriculum to a theme, says educator Ann Litzler Coyne, author of the delightful *Creating a Year-Long Theme: A Teacher's Journey* (2000). For instance, Coyne once adopted a circus theme for a combined third- and fourth-grade classroom. "I did the circus because I looked at the different topics we were studying, and there were things like the human body," she recalls. "So I related that back to the circus—the agility and the flexibility that you need as a performer, and the different muscle groups you use. We also had to study regions of the United States, so we tracked Ringling Bros. Circus on the map as they went all around the country. We'd also be reading the textbook and studying different areas, but we related everything back to the circus. We had pen pals with people who were in a smaller circus."

The circus tie-ins got even more creative as the year progressed. "In science, we had a unit on pendulums and we related that back to the elephant's trunk swinging back and forth and how the trapeze swings back and forth," Coyne notes. "Math easily fit into the theme. We made juggling balls one day and filled some with rice, some with birdseed, and some with sand, and we measured out the differences."

The experience energized Coyne as well as her students: "The thing that I liked about it was, not only was it engaging for the students—I set up my classroom so it looked like a circus; my library corner had a big top above it—but it was fun to teach that way. And it gave an extra purpose to the whole year." The circus antics even spurred great cross-curricular cooperation. "The specialty teachers were excited about the theme, because no one ever really talked to them about what was going on in the classroom," Coyne recalls. "The music teacher ended up helping me put on an entire circus-type musical. And the gym teacher helped me by turning different circus acts into a physical education unit—balancing on the balance beam and all that kind of stuff. It just feeds on itself."

Even so, she cautions against trying to link every aspect of the curriculum to a theme. "There are some things that don't fit," Coyne says. "I had to teach a program on gang awareness, and that didn't fit in. And if something doesn't fit, don't force it. But try and find a theme that will fit most of the big topics you have to cover during the year. . . . Plan on at least 15 to 20 hours over the summer figuring out how you're going to implement it."

5. Build excitement throughout the year. In addition to tying lesson plans into the theme, it's important to give students regular updates about the progress they're making toward their overall academic goal—and reminders of how much they must accomplish in the remaining time to set the stunt into motion. Include updates in morning announcements. Set up an exhibit in a central area to track the academic progress. Some principals even maintain focus by performing smaller stunts throughout the year as students hit milestones on the way to the larger educational goal. It's crucial to maintain parent support for stunts as well. Do this by providing regular updates about student progress toward the achievement goal on the school Web site and in communications sent home. If you'll be wearing a silly costume for the stunt, include a picture of you trying it on in the parent newsletter. And consider performing a lead-in stunt for parents and students at a back-to-school night at mid-year.

6. Alert the media. TV and newspaper reporters eat up motivational stunt stories. They provide an interesting, highly photogenic hook for reporting good news about educational achievement. Turn to Chapter 5 for expert tips on generating great coverage for your performance.

7. Plan an encore. Keep the excitement alive and the educational gains growing by turning the motivational stunt into an annual tradition at your school.

3 Silly Suggestions, Boffo Blueprints, and Idiotic Ideas

101 Stunts That Will Motivate Your Students to New Academic Heights

In the following pages, I'll outline 101 stunts that adventurous educators can employ to inspire and motivate students to higher academic achievement. Although a few of the suggestions may be new to the school setting, most of these stunts have been used successfully to meet educational goals. In fact, I'll share dozens of "success snapshots" culled from exclusive educator interviews and media accounts of stunts gone right.

After describing each stunt, I'll offer suggestions for related cross-curricular activities, tips for avoiding problems, additional resources worth exploring, and references to complementary stunts in the book so you can mix and match them to your heart's—and your students'—delight.

STUNTS FOR EVERY OCCASION

Many of the stunts lend themselves to quick and easy execution. These are perfect for rewarding students after they meet short-term goals—or for combining with other simple stunts into a larger performance. However, several of the activities require quite a bit of preparation, group effort, and even assistance from outside experts such as magicians and animal trainers. Save these more complex stunts for celebrations of major student achievements.

WHAT'S YOUR SILLINESS QUOTIENT?

Every educator has a different comfort level when it comes to being silly in public, and every student population has unique motivational needs. So I've given each stunt a Silliness Rating of 1–5 (with 1 being the tamest), as well as a Gross-Out Rating of 1–5. With 101 options at varying levels of silliness and gross-out potential, it shouldn't be too difficult to find several that will meet the needs of your students while fitting snugly into your comfort zone. Remember, though, that stretching beyond your comfort level is a great way to foster personal and professional growth. And realize that many educators who become addicted to motivational stunts soon find themselves on a never-ending quest to top the previous year's performance.

STUNTS SECOND, SAFETY FIRST

An important note regarding danger: This book avoids potentially dangerous stunts that students could too easily attempt. The following pages do not outline stunts that involve jumping through flaming hoops, swallowing fire, or walking on hot coals, for instance. However, some of the stunts—such as skydiving, wrestling an alligator, or moving your office to the school roof—do present potential dangers to you. Although students likely won't have the ready means to duplicate those stunts, no one wants you to get hurt, either. So please secure professional assistance whenever warranted, and always put safety first when attempting even the simplest stunt. After all, getting hit in the face with a pie is only fun until the chocolate shavings scratch a cornea. When in doubt, opt for protective gear such as goggles—and clothes you don't mind throwing away.

Once that sobering message has sunk in, read on to get silly once again.

No. 1: The Razor's Edge

Silliness Rating: 3
Gross-Out Rating: 1
Mix-and-Match Possibilities: Stunts Nos. 26, 100

Basic Stunt: Have your head shaved during a special assembly

FRILLS, CHILLS, & SPILLS

- Male educators can opt to shave off their beards and/or mustaches instead. This works especially well when the facial hair has been a trademark feature for many years. The bigger the sacrifice you make, the more impressive the stunt will be. Trimming a month-old goatee isn't very inspirational—but shaving your furry legs might be.
- Instead of going bald, consider shaving the school initials into your hair.
- Heighten the fun by enlisting a student or two as barber's assistants.
- Borrow a barber chair and craft a candy-striped pole to make the event seem more "official."
- Ask a fellow faculty or staff member to dress up as a famous stylist and turn the haircut into a theatrical happening. Or perform an excerpt of *The Barber of Seville*. If it was good enough for Bugs Bunny and Elmer Fudd, it'll probably work for you.
- Play hair-related songs over the PA system, such as the title song of the flower-child musical *Hair*, "I Dream of Jeannie with the Light Brown Hair," America's "Sister Golden Hair," Everclear's "Short Blonde Hair," and "Almost Cut My Hair" from Crosby, Stills, Nash, and Young. Unfortunately, the Weird Al Yankovic album *Bad Hair Day* has no actual songs about hair, but you'll undoubtedly find a few more—such as George Thorogood's "Get a Haircut," and Ray Stevens' "The Haircut Song"—if you comb your memory.
- Bring in several silly hats and ask students to vote on which one you'll wear for the rest of the day after going bald.

LEARNING LINKS

- Develop a math unit exploring such hair-raising statistics as the average number of hairs on a human head and the average price for a haircut at local salons. Do activities related to zero, noting that the number looks just like a bald head.
- Create a natural science and geography unit on bald eagles. Compare nature's most hirsute creatures with naturally hairless ones.
- Make hats and hair adornments in art class.
- Ask students to write essays and stories about how going bald would affect their lives. Read and perform the Rapunzel fairytale.
- Devote a health unit to good grooming habits and maintaining healthy hair.

OBSTACLE AVOIDANCE

- Make sure your significant other will let you back in the house after you've been shorn.
- If a member of the school community has recently lost his or her hair as a result of cancer treatments, consider shaving your head as a show of solidarity rather than doing it as part of a motivational stunt.

SUCCESS SNAPSHOTS

- After a Read a Million challenge prompted students at Annapolis, Maryland's Edgewater Elementary to pore over a million book pages during the school year, a parent volunteer shaved Principal Barry J. Fader's head during an assembly. After Fader lost his locks, an art teacher painted the school's eagle mascot on his bald dome. "It is about making kids eager to read both here at school and at home," the principal told *The Capital*. "I walked from class to class after the assembly, and they were all reading" (Furgurson, 1999).
- Capping off a successful fundraiser to replace a 40-year-old gymnasium floor, the principal of Racine, Wisconsin's Gifford Elementary was shaved bald and lost his mustache during a student assembly marked by chants of "Cut it! Cut it! Cut it!" Steve Russo spent the week before the stunt toting a hand mirror around the school for frequent checks of his thick, wavy locks. Fifteen young barbers—students whose families raised more than $100 for the project—took turns with the clippers. The stunt helped bring in $6,000, well above

the goal of $4,000. "I see how hard the kids work in school every day, so this is my way of giving back," Russo told the *Milwaukee Journal Sentinel.* "With the lack of money in the school districts, you kind of have to be thinking outside the box" (Sweeney, 2004).

- When students blew by their goal of reading 15,000 books by the end of the school year, Glenn Aguiar, principal of Meridian, Idaho's Mary McPherson Elementary, shaved his head more than two months ahead of schedule. Under the direction of a local stylist, kids who had racked up the most Accelerated Reader points helped shave Aguiar's head as 600 other students cheered. "It's fun, it didn't cost a dime, and it motivated them to read," the principal crowed to the *Idaho Statesman.* Earlier, Aguiar told his students, "Just because I'm losing my hair, I don't want to lose your respect. I respect you and I expect you to respect me" (Mortensen, 2000).

- Selling his facial hair cheap, Principal Mark Soss shaved off the beard he'd been sporting for nearly 30 years after 650 students at Chappaqua, New York's Roaring Brook Elementary agreed to avoid TV for three days. The *shear* madness took place at an assembly marking the successful completion of the local PTA's "Cold Turkey TV Turnoff" initiative. Kids signed contracts with parents promising to turn off the tube, abstain from video games, and surf the Web only for homework research. "It's an incentive for the kids and a real school morale builder. This group of children and half of my staff has never seen me without the beard," Soss told *The Journal News* of Westchester County. "Almost every child has participated in the 'TV Turnoff' to some point. We produced lists of activities they could do with their families—like reading and games—to keep them away from TV and electronic games and concentrate on constructive activities. It shows them that life without TV is not the end of the world. There actually are other things you can do" (Gorman, 2002).

No. 2: Book the Bookmobile

Silliness Rating: 1
Gross-Out Rating: 1
Mix-and-Match Possibilities: Stunts Nos. 25, 49, 66, 71, 74

Basic Stunt: Spend the day distributing books from the local public library's bookmobile

FRILLS, CHILLS, & SPILLS

- Add excitement by holding a celebration in the school parking lot before embarking on your route.
- Consider riding atop the bookmobile, or at least driving it around the lot—perhaps dressed in a costume with a literary theme.
- Adorn the bookmobile with construction paper "book covers" featuring the names of classes or individual students, noting how many pages or books they read during the challenge period.
- Hand out commemorative bookmarks to everyone in attendance. Invite top readers to accompany you on at least part of your bookmobile odyssey.

LEARNING LINKS

- This stunt ties in beautifully with reading-related goals.
- Integrate bookmobile details into math problems, using figures such as the length of its route, the number of miles it travels each year, the amount of gas it consumes, and the number of books it distributes.
- In addition to this stunt's obvious language arts links, it also lends itself well to a social studies unit on the history of libraries in general and bookmobiles specifically. For instance, students will be interested to discover the first U.S. bookmobile was a "bookwagon" that bounced along the roads of Washington County, Maryland, way back in 1905.

OBSTACLE AVOIDANCE

- Get the school librarian involved in the early planning stages of this stunt. The librarian will likely be able to help with public library outreach and will have plenty of ideas for tying the event into the curriculum.
- If you do ride atop the bookmobile, make sure you're strapped on tight and have a safe place to dismount. Practice a few times before the kids arrive.

SUCCESS SNAPSHOT

- Ellis Elementary in Round Lake, Illinois, partnered with the local public library to make the school a regular stop on the bookmobile's route. Students received special library cards enabling them to check out any of the 3,000-plus books housed in the repurposed yellow school bus, which fits right in on campus. "Promoting a love of reading and a love of stories is important, whether or not it translates to a test," Principal Ben Rosenfield told the *Chicago Daily Herald*. "The more we enjoy reading and the more it touches us, the better off we are. I'm sure it'll help. This is an opportunity that I couldn't provide any other way" (King, 2003).

CURRICULUM RESOURCES

Chupela, D. (1994). *Ready, set, go!: Children's programming for bookmobiles and other small spaces*. Fort Atkinson, WI: Highsmith.
Levinson, N. S. (1988). *Clara and the bookwagon*. New York: HarperCollins Juvenile.

No. 3: Play Dead

Silliness Rating: 2
Gross-Out Rating: 3
Mix-and-Match Possibilities: Stunt No. 25

Basic Stunt: Play the dead body during a *CSI*-style murder mystery event

FRILLS, CHILLS, & SPILLS

- Enlist good-humored faculty and staff members to play nefarious suspects. Concoct several silly motives to throw students off the scent.
- Set a realistic scene by using white medical tape to create a "chalk" outline of the body. Rope off the area with crime-scene tape borrowed from local police.
- Whip up a batch of movie-style fake blood. Mix one cup of light corn syrup with a tablespoon of water, two tablespoons of red food coloring, and one tablespoon of yellow food coloring.
- Make it a family affair by inviting parents to participate with their kids in a full-blown mystery evening.

LEARNING LINKS

- Base a science unit on crime-solving techniques ranging from fingerprinting to fiber analysis. Study the history of investigative methods as well.
- Encourage students to read and write mysteries for language arts.
- Help kids hone their logic skills with afterschool games of Clue.
- Create geometry worksheets with a crime-scene theme.

OBSTACLE AVOIDANCE

- Involve the drama instructor in planning—and executing—this stunt. The more realistic your "corpse" looks, the more memorable this stunt will be.
- Wear clothes you won't mind throwing away if the gore gets too messy.
- Pick a comfortable position. You're going to be there a while.

SUCCESS SNAPSHOTS

- A Murder Mystery Night at Pinckneyville, Georgia's Pinckneyville Middle School brought students and parents in on the investigative act. Teachers invited a local homicide detective to preside over the event, which featured a mock crime scene complete with odd stains, the outline of a body, and mysterious animal prints. "We want them to understand that forensic scientists and police officers really use the concepts that they are studying," science instructor Linda Flagler told the *Atlanta Journal-Constitution*. Students conducted 10 scientific tests on the evidence—including discerning the acidity of liquids and examining fabric samples—and considered statements from four suspects before formulating a theory about who committed the murder. In the end, none of the kids or parents could say with certainty who did the dastardly deed. "But you got a chance to see how science works in real life," Flagler told them (Mungin, 2003).
- A murder mystery day at Greensboro, North Carolina's Mendenhall Middle School capped off a cross-curricular project on mystery solving led by language-arts teacher Sharon Guhman, math teacher Melanie Hitt, and social studies instructor Juan Fernandez. With teachers playing the roles of suspects and parents helping out with props, the costumed children participated in a mystery set at a high school reunion. The scenario came from one of the popular How to Host a Murder Mystery kits. "Creative projects like this help the students reach beyond a pencil and paper level of learning,"

Guhman told the *Greensboro News & Record*. "Educational activities such as this are important for building life skills like cooperation, team building, and problem solving" (Brown, 2000).

CURRICULUM RESOURCES

Boland, M. A. (2003). *Mystery disease.* San Luis Obispo, CA: Dandy Lion.

Carr, M. A. (1992). *The great chocolate caper: A mystery that teaches logic skills.* San Luis Obispo, CA: Dandy Lion.

Carr, M. A. (1994). *One-hour mysteries.* San Luis Obispo, CA: Dandy Lion.

Gatlin, C. (2002). *Mystery science: Case of the missing lunch.* San Luis Obispo, CA: Dandy Lion.

Gannon, M. B. (2004). *Blood, bedlam, bullets, and badguys: A reader's guide to adventure/ suspense fiction.* Westport, CT: Libraries Unlimited.

Schulz, K. (2003). *Crime scene detective: Using science and critical thinking to solve crimes.* San Luis Obispo, CA: Dandy Lion.

No. 4: Cheer Up!

Silliness Rating: 3
Gross-Out Rating: 1
Mix-and-Match Possibilities:
Stunts Nos. 7, 18, 84

Basic Stunt: Become a school cheerleader for a day

FRILLS, CHILLS, & SPILLS

- You're probably already your school's biggest cheerleader, so why not grab a set of pom-poms and make it official?
- Although you might send students into a frenzy simply by donning a cheerleading uniform, this stunt will prove much more memorable if you perform a simple routine or two—preferably as part of the squad.

LEARNING LINKS

- Ask the P.E. teacher to develop a fun cheerleading workout that all students can use to get fit.

OBSTACLE AVOIDANCE

- Enlist the support of the cheerleading coach—and the cheerleaders themselves—to give you a leg up on this stunt.
- Explain that you'll be having fun with your own image, not making fun of their activity.

SUCCESS SNAPSHOT

- LeJay Graffious established a Summer Reading Challenge at Bruceton Mills, West Virginia's Bruceton Elementary when he became principal in 1994. Every year, Graffious performed a motivational stunt to encourage student reading. The first time out, he dressed up as Mother Goose. In subsequent years, he rode a mule through town, had himself planted in the ground as a human tree next to a local bank president, let kids turn him into a human sundae, dined on a meal of worms, became a "monkey's uncle" with simian in tow, played a cheerleader for a day, and let students douse him with colorful "slime." Graffious left the school for another principalship at the end of 2001, but he's proud to note that his annual stunts helped motivate Bruceton students to read nearly 2.5 million pages over eight summers.

SOURCE: E-mail communication with LeJay Graffious, January 18, 2004.

CURRICULUM RESOURCES

Neil, R., & Hart E. (1986). *The official cheerleader's handbook.* New York: Fireside.

No. 5: Robot Wars

Silliness Rating: 2
Gross-Out Rating: 1
Mix-and-Match Possibilities: Stunts Nos. 29, 86

Basic Stunt: Participate in a robotics unit that culminates in robot races or a gladiator-style demolition derby

FRILLS, CHILLS, & SPILLS

- Brush off your old school moves and do a robot dance to kick off the big event.
- Dress up as Data from the *Star Trek* films and become an android administrator for the day.

LEARNING LINKS

- Although this is a hard-core science and math project, it can forge connections across the curriculum. Focus reading assignments on YA science fiction stories, for instance.
- Plug art into the process by asking students to sketch robot designs and decorate the operating models.

OBSTACLE AVOIDANCE

- Conduct several dry runs to make sure your robot won't spin in circles at the starting line.

SUCCESS SNAPSHOT

- Some 1,400 students on 57 teams participated in the Southern California FIRST Robotics Competition for a shot at the nationals in 2004. With more than 20,000 teens competing in 26 regional heats nationwide, it's clear that robotics is a great way to spark student interest in math and science. Robots compete by lifting inflatable balls, executing climbing maneuvers, and even completing chin-ups in timed heats. Palm Desert, California's Palm Desert High team, the Aztechs, won their regional event in 2003 on their first attempt. "This program brings together mentors, professionals, the teachers, college students, and high school students on one team," Palm Desert senior Felipe Nelson told the *Desert Sun*. "It brings everything that you learn in school into one place, over six weeks, in compressed time." Winning teams can spend more than 200 hours building and testing their robots. For more details on the main competition and a junior version that uses Lego® blocks, visit the FIRST Robotics Web site at (http://www.usfirst.org/.) By the way, that acronym translates to For Inspiration and Recognition of Science and Technology (Perrault, 2004).

CURRICULUM RESOURCES

Gurstelle, W. (2002). *Building bots: Designing and building warrior robots.* Chicago: Chicago Review Press.

Hannold, C. (2002). *Combat robots complete: Everything you need to build, compete, and win.* New York: McGraw-Hill.

Imahara, G. (2003). *Kickin' bot: An illustrated guide to building combat robots.* New York: John Wiley.

Iovine, J. (2001). *Robots, androids and animatrons: 12 incredible projects you can build* (2nd ed.). New York: McGraw-Hill.

Miles, P., & Carroll, T. (2002). *Build your own combat robot.* New York: McGraw-Hill.

No. 6: Bug Buffet

Silliness Rating: 4
Gross-Out Rating: 5
Mix-and-Match Possibilities: Stunts Nos. 13, 100

Basic Stunt: Make a meal of mealworms

FRILLS, CHILLS, & SPILLS

- Instead of popping live bait into your mouth, take the gourmet route. Consider sampling the following recipes for Mealworm Fried Rice and Earthworm Noodles.

Mealworm Fried Rice

Ingredients: 1 egg, 1 tsp. oil, ¾ c. water, ¼ c. chopped onions, 4 tsp. soy sauce, 1/8 tsp. garlic powder, 1 c. minute rice, 1 c. cooked mealworms

Directions: Scramble the egg in a hot saucepan. Add water, soy sauce, garlic powder, and onions. Bring to a boil. Stir in rice. Cover, remove from heat, and let stand for five minutes. Top with cooked mealworms.

Earthworm Noodles

Ingredients: 1½ lb. earthworms, ½ large onion, ¼ c. chicken bouillon, 1 c. sour cream, 3 Tb. butter, whole wheat flour, ½ c. mushrooms (optional).

Directions: Wash the earthworms thoroughly. Purge the worms by boiling them three times and then baking them at 350 degrees for 15 minutes. Coat the cleaned and purged worms and brown them in butter, salting to taste. Add bouillon and simmer for 30 minutes, stirring occasionally. Chop the onion and sauté it with the mushrooms in butter. Add both to the earthworms. Stir in sour cream. Serve over chow mein noodles.

LEARNING LINKS

- This stunt provides a smorgasbord of opportunities for natural science instruction, from basic bug biology to the role worms play in the composting process.
- As part of a social studies project, explore cultures that regularly eat larvae and other insect life.
- Use an insect menu as a springboard into a nutrition discussion about the importance of different protein sources to a healthy diet.
- Access state-of-the-art microscope views of various insects live online through the Bugscope program offered by the Beckman Institute for Advanced Science and Technology at the University of Illinois. For full details, visit http://bugscope.beckman.uiuc.edu.

OBSTACLE AVOIDANCE

- Check with an entomologist at a local university whenever you're unsure if a particularly squirmy menu item is safe to ingest.
- If children protest the eating of bugs on humanitarian grounds, turn their concerns into a teachable moment. For instance, one of the following schools held student debates on the issue and then took a schoolwide vote before going forward with the stunt.

SUCCESS SNAPSHOTS

- Principal Rob Hanson promised to eat a cricket in front of all students at Rochester, New Hampshire's William Allen Elementary who met a monthly reading goal. Ten of 15 classes hit the mark, so they got to enjoy the icky performance in the cafeteria. The principal chowed down on the cricket as part of a district program called 90 Percent Reading Goal that aims to have 9 out of 10 third graders reading at grade level. Going by a list of student suggestions, Hanson completed a similarly silly stunt every month in 2003–2004. But swallowing a cricket easily topped dyeing his hair purple on the gross-out scale. "The worst part of it was when he went to the back of my throat and wouldn't go down," Hanson told the Associated Press ("Principal eats crickets . . .", 2004).

- When students at Bucks County, Pennsylvania's Makefield Elementary served Principal Donna McCormick-Miller a lunch of banana worm bread, mealworm fried rice, and worm stroganoff, she graciously sampled it all. She dined on the squirmy meal during an assembly in the school auditorium, after the 435 K-5 students read 5,000 books in three months. The mealworms tasted like roasted peanuts. The earthworms in the stroganoff, however, were hard to distinguish from the mushrooms. "There is not another principal in the district who would do this," local PTO President Heather Humienny said, adding that McCormick-Miller "has made this school soar" (*News in brief from the Philadelphia area, 2001*).

- Downing three live mealworms was a delight for Principal Shirley DiRado after her stunt helped double participation in the annual Read-a-Thon at L.A.'s Colfax Avenue Elementary. As a bonus, media outlets from as far away as South Africa covered the event. "It got kids to read who normally wouldn't be interested," DiRado told the *L.A. Times*. "Parents were calling and saying, 'I can't believe it. They want to read.'" However, the principal added, "I'm not going to do this every year" (Bailey, 2002).

- Earthworms weren't an easy meal choice for Principal Rob Elkins and Assistant Principal Ralph Wade at Newport, North Carolina's Newport Elementary. Sure, the squirmers are none too appetizing. But after promising to eat worms if K-5 students earned 18,000 Accelerated Reader points, Elkins and Wade also had to cope with a protest over the stunt launched by fifth graders who wanted to let the creatures live. Seizing the opportunity to teach a lesson in democracy, the administrators let students take a vote to decide the worms' fate. During the ensuing campaign, kids debated the issue, calculated how many votes would win the day, wrote position papers, and even studied worm biology. After losing 560–335, the wigglers were cooked and served at a school assembly. "Anyone that can eat an oyster ought to be able to eat a worm," Elkins told the *Raleigh News & Observer* (Allegood, 1998).

- A full five-course meal of bugs awaited Principal Alan Cook after students at Orangevale, California's Green Oaks Fundamental Elementary met a schoolwide reading goal. With the help of an entomologist from the University of California-Davis, staffers cooked up creepy delights ranging from mealworm pâté on toast points to bacon-wrapped crickets. At least Cook's table was set with a fine linen tablecloth and crystal stemware—not to mention a "barf bucket" done up in sparkly gold lamé. "It was gross," Cook told the *L.A. Times*. "I felt like using the bucket, but I couldn't in front of all those kids" (Hwangbo, 1994).

CURRICULUM RESOURCES

Facklam, M. (1999). *Bugs for lunch.* Watertown, MA: Charlesbridge Publishing.
Gordon, D. G. (1998). *Eat-a-bug cookbook.* Berkeley, CA: Ten Speed Press.
Menzel, P. (1998). *Man eating bugs: The art and science of eating insects.* Berkeley, CA: Ten Speed Press.
Ramos-Elorduy, J. (1998). *Creepy crawly cuisine: The gourmet guide to edible insects.* Rochester, VT: Park Street Press.
Rockwell, T. (1953). *How to eat fried worms.* New York: Yearling Books.
Schwabe, C. W. (1988). *Unmentionable cuisine.* Charlottesville, VA: University of Virginia Press.

No. 7: Mascot Mayhem

Silliness Rating: 4
Gross-Out Rating: 1
Mix-and-Match Possibilities: Stunts Nos. 4, 10, 84

Basic Stunt: Dress up as your school's mascot for the day

FRILLS, CHILLS, & SPILLS

- Perform a funny athletic routine at a special assembly or on the sidelines of the big game.

LEARNING LINKS

- Devote a cross-curricular unit to studying the animal or figure your school mascot represents, whether it's a wildcat or a Viking.

OBSTACLE AVOIDANCE

- If your mascot is a Native American symbol, doing this stunt might inflame community opinion against it.

SUCCESS SNAPSHOT

- When students at Chapel Hill, North Carolina's Estes Hills Elementary met a service-learning goal, Principal Dale Minge did more than just climb into the school's eagle mascot costume. He also climbed onto the roof in the suit and serenaded students with the school song. "It's nice for children to laugh and see me in a nontraditional manner," Minge told the *Raleigh News & Observer.* "It makes me more approachable to kids. I want kids to see me as more than the principal holed up in his office" (Reddy, 2000).

No. 8: Clown Around

Silliness Rating: 5
Gross-Out Rating: 2
Mix-and-Match Possibilities: Stunts Nos. 12, 15, 28, 32, 78, 94

Basic Stunt: Show up at school decked out as a circus clown

FRILLS, CHILLS, & SPILLS

- Enlist fellow educators and staff members to dress up as clowns and pack as many of them as possible into a designated "clown car" during a special assembly.
- Perform a juggling act, and practice feats of clown magic such as pulling an endless string of colored handkerchiefs out of your sleeve.

LEARNING LINKS

- Adopt a circus theme for as many lessons as possible. For instance, natural science units could focus on circus animals, while math lessons could rely on everything from figuring distances that circuses cover to determining the number of clowns that can fit into a Volkswagen Beetle.

OBSTACLE AVOIDANCE

- Because very young children are sometimes afraid of clowns, this stunt might not work well for the preschool and kindergarten set.

SUCCESS SNAPSHOT

- Every year, Principal Nancy Rials promises to complete a silly stunt if students at Forest Hill, Louisiana's Forest Hill Elementary hit a specified reading goal. The only catch: She doesn't get to find out exactly what the stunt will be until she has to perform it. (Other adults are in on the planning to make sure the task is reasonable.) One year, Rials found herself parading around the halls dressed as a clown, from colorful wig and crazy makeup right down to a pair of giant shoes. Luckily, Rials usually gets a few hints about what to expect. For instance, that year's reading theme was "Don't Clown Around." As school librarian Kimberly Duck told the *Alexandria Daily Town Talk* of the principal, "She's just a real, real good sport" (Gregory, 1999).

CURRICULUM RESOURCES

Burk, M. C. (2002). *Station games: Fun and imaginative PE lessons.* Champaign, IL: Human Kinetics.

Fife, B., Blanco, T., Kissell, S., & Harris, E. (1992). *Creative clowning.* Colorado Springs, CO: Piccadilly Books.

Coyne, A. L. (2000). *Creating a year-long theme: A teacher's journey.* Columbus, OH: Englefield & Arnold.

No. 9: Marathon Plan

Silliness Rating: 1
Gross-Out Rating: 1
Mix-and-Match Possibilities: Stunt No. 66

Basic Stunt: Promise to run a marathon if students meet a long-term educational goal

FRILLS, CHILLS, & SPILLS

- As you train, encourage walking by regularly leading a "human school bus" to campus along a set route. Enlist parents or other volunteers to bring up the rear.
- As students hit various milestones *en route* to reaching their main goal, participate in corresponding 5k and 10k runs.

LEARNING LINKS

- This stunt will tie in especially well to P.E. and math units.
- Exploit the service-learning opportunities of a marathon run by raising money for charity with your effort. For instance, Team in Training, the world's largest endurance sports training program, provides excellent support for first-time marathoners while raising money for the Leukemia & Lymphoma Society. Find out more at http://www.teamintraining.org.

OBSTACLE AVOIDANCE

- If you've never run a marathon, talk to your doctor before adopting a training regimen.

SUCCESS SNAPSHOT

- Six elementary principals from California's Garden Grove Unified School District banded together to train for the Los Angeles Marathon in both 2003 and 2004. Event organizers dubbed the team "The Running Principals," naturally enough. The administrators found many similarities between training for an endurance race and running a school. "You always have to pace yourself," Thomas Paine Elementary Principal Beth Cusimano told the *L.A. Daily News.* "There's sort of the same psychological aspect to both. You might be going on a 20-mile run one day or have a big meeting the next." If you do choose to reward students by running a marathon, consider joining other administrators in getting up to speed (Siler, 2004).

CURRICULUM RESOURCES

Decker, J., & Mize, M. (2002). *Walking games and activities.* Champaign, IL: Human Kinetics.

Whitsett, D. A. (1998). *The non-runner's marathon trainer.* Chicago: Contemporary Books.

No. 10: Hit the Roof

Silliness Rating: 5
Gross-Out Rating: 1
Mix-and-Match Possibilities: Stunts Nos. 7, 22, 29, 30, 38, 49

Basic Stunt: Move your office to the school roof

FRILLS, CHILLS, & SPILLS

- Tie the educational goal directly to the promised stunt with a slogan such as "Reading Takes You to New Heights" or "The Sky's the Limit on Test Scores."
- Consider reading the morning announcements over a megaphone.
- Volunteer to monitor the playground from on high during recess.
- Instead of moving your office to the roof, pitch a tent instead and camp there overnight.

LEARNING LINKS

- Create a math unit that will help you figure out the logistics of moving your office to the roof.

OBSTACLE AVOIDANCE

- Dress for the weather, stay away from the roof edge during windy weather, and don't forget sunblock.

SUCCESS SNAPSHOTS

- After 581 students at Gustafson Elementary in Batavia, Illinois, read more than 450,000 pages over an eight-week span, Principal Alan McCloud spent a full day on the school roof as part of a "Reach for the Stars" initiative dreamed up by Carol Sturz, learning resource center director. Preparing for the stunt meant spending a Sunday maneuvering a desk and other necessities—ranging from a computer, phone, and office fern to a tent, clothes rack, and barbecue grill—atop the building. Then, with only the aid of a wading pool and a bottle of sunblock, McCloud braved 80-degree temperatures to spend the next Monday high above his delighted students. In the morning, he shouted the school announcements down to them. At recess, he dressed as Superman and watched over the playground. Later in the day, he grilled up hot dogs for the faculty and staff. That evening, he camped out under the stars. Halfway through the two-month reading period, McCloud had given the kids a pep talk that prompted them to beat their 400,000-page goal. "I was surprised they were able to stick to it," the principal told the *Chicago Tribune.* "The carrot was appropriate, but I thought an eight-week program was way too long for them to maintain interest. But once we got to the halfway point and we put it up on the board, it really took off." Added McCloud, "Most principals would have chosen to sit on the roof all day if they thought it would motivate children to read" (Young, 1992).

- Spending a December day atop his school was not what Principal Andre Assalian had in mind when he challenged the 1,100 students at Alexandria, Virginia's Francis C. Hammond Junior High to read a million pages by March. But after they attained their goal several months early, Assalian donned gloves and thermal underwear and kept his part of the bargain. The local fire department arrived in the morning to lift him onto the roof in a cherry picker while the school band played "Anchors Aweigh." During the day, the principal communicated with his secretary via walkie-talkie, read notes passed up by students, welcomed visiting school board members, and ate a cold turkey lunch that was supposed to be hot. "This is the easiest part," Assalian told the *Washington Times.* "What the students did is day in and day out" (Metzler, 1992).

- Principal Jack Giordano bounded onto the roof after the 450 students of Windham, Connecticut's North Windham Elementary collectively read for 25,000 hours at home during the school year. For his 2.5-hour stint atop the school, Giordano donned walking shorts and a straw hat. Capping off a "Reading . . . The Great Escape" initiative, he jumped rope and used everything from bent wire hangers and six-pack rings to send giant soap bubbles soaring over the grounds, the *Hartford Courant* reported. Individual classrooms earned rewards as well. For instance, guest authors visited classes whose students had logged more than 1,750 hours of leisure-time reading (Tarr, 1994).

- Principal Tom Rodriguez tied his motivational stunt into National Reading Month, promising the 400 students at East Lansing, Michigan's Pinecrest Elementary he'd spend a morning on the roof if they read on their own time for 2,000 hours one March. When the kids hit their mark, so did Rodriguez, who in other years has kissed pigs, cut up his necktie, spent a day as a silent clown, and granted wishes dressed as a prince. This time around, the principal dressed in school colors—green and white—and took a cherry-picker ride onto the roof, where he held court for three hours in a rocking chair bedecked with a school flag. Students and teachers offered him treats that he pulled up in a bucket tied to a rope. The kids also got hourly reports from Rodriguez over the school's closed-circuit TV system. Afterwards, one third grader told the *Lansing State Journal*, "It's funner to read when you get something special at the end" (Mayes, 1999).

- Principal Ken Morr started the school year in a lawn chair atop Florissant, Missouri's St. Dismas School after his K-8 students met their summer goal of reading 15 or more books each. "I'm willing to try anything, because . . . getting kids to read is the most important thing," Morr told the *St. Louis Post-Dispatch*. "A lot of people are getting a kick out of it. It lets the kids see a different side of you. It's nice to have that happen." Added Morr, "It's a fact that reading is proven to be one of the most educationally sound things a child can do. In the future, no matter what it is, as long as it helps the kids out, I'm willing to do it" (Harris, 2002).

No. 11: Trading Places

Silliness Rating: 3
Gross-Out Rating: 1
Mix-and-Match Possibilities: Stunts Nos. 54, 64

Basic Stunt: Swap jobs with a teacher, coach, or staff member for a day

FRILLS, CHILLS, & SPILLS

- Let students select who you'll switch jobs with through a special election.
- Pick a highly visible task so the children will get plenty of chances to see you in action.

LEARNING LINKS

- Hold a career fair in conjunction with your stunt.

OBSTACLE AVOIDANCE

- Be careful not to say or do anything that demeans the job you take on, whether it's mopping floors as a janitor, dishing up spuds as a lunchroom server, or coaching the football team.

SUCCESS SNAPSHOT

- Principal Nicholas Maldonado traded his desk for a mop when he swapped jobs for a day with custodian Kim Trauth at Mark Twain School in Niles, Illinois. They made the switch after students met a reading goal. The pair learned a lot about each other's jobs—and gave students some interesting career insights. "I have always had the understanding that I need to motivate children to read after school because I am in direct competition with television," Maldonado told the *Niles Herald-Spectator.* "I instituted the reading challenge so kids could get the understanding that I am willing to do anything to get them to read" (Johnson, 2004).

CURRICULUM RESOURCES

JIST Editors. (2003). *Exploring careers: A young person's guide to 1,000 jobs* (3rd ed.). Indianapolis, IN: JIST Publishing.

No. 12: Crossed-Up Crossing Guard

Silliness Rating: 4
Gross-Out Rating: 1
Mix-and-Match Possibilities: Stunts Nos. 4, 7, 8, 15, 18, 22, 29, 49

Basic Stunt: Direct traffic at school dressed in silly garb

FRILLS, CHILLS, & SPILLS

- Add some physical comedy to the mix by making exaggerated hand gestures as you bring parents' cars in for a landing as if they're jumbo jets.

LEARNING LINKS

- Take a serious look at traffic safety in connection with this stunt.

OBSTACLE AVOIDANCE

- Ask the police department to park a squad car in clear view a few blocks from school on the morning of your stunt so that parents are on their best behavior by the time they pull into your traffic circle.

SUCCESS SNAPSHOTS

- Principal Gregory Decker saluted the academic achievements of students at Raleigh, North Carolina's Lead Mine Elementary by directing traffic at the school one morning garbed in a wet suit, goggles, snorkel, and, of course, flippers. Decker told the *Raleigh News and Observer*, "If we can find some incentive and have some fun and give kids something to shoot for, along with a sense of empowerment, then why not?"
- Jenda Turner can really stop traffic. The principal of San Juan Capistrano, California's Rancho Capistrano Christian School rewarded students for reaching a fundraising goal by greeting them one morning dressed in pajamas and curlers. "When I was standing there, a lot of parents couldn't see who I was, and so were speeding up to drive past, probably thinking I was some crazy person," Turner recalls with a chuckle. "I actually walked around the rest of the day in my pajamas and curlers." She adds, "The principal's office should hold respect, but at the same time I want students to know that my most important job is to mentor them and to listen to them, and that's largely what I do inside my office. I'm a hands-on principal anyway, but the fact that I was goofy with them humanized me and was meaningful to them. I don't rule by fear. You certainly can do that, but I don't think in the long run that that's very successful. I don't think you create any great memories when you do that."

SOURCE: Telephone interview with Jenda Turner, September 26, 2003.

No. 13: Pucker Up

Silliness Rating: 5
Gross-Out Rating: 4
Mix-and-Match Possibilities: Stunts Nos. 6, 37, 48, 63, 87, 100

Basic Stunt: Kiss a pig or other animal

FRILLS, CHILLS, & SPILLS

- Add as many wacky touches as you can think of to make the experience more memorable for students. For instance, when an Ohio assistant principal set out to reward students by locking lips with a hog, the school changed its reader-board message from "Board Meeting" to "Pig Kissing Day," and staffers all hammed it up by wearing rubber pig snouts for the big event.
- Build excitement—and get big laughs—with a false start. If you promise to kiss a pig or a cow, bring out a plastic version first. When the students howl in protest, move on to the real thing.

LEARNING LINKS

- Adopt a farming theme for the year and tie it in to all academic areas.
- Focus a natural science unit on the animal you'll be smooching.

OBSTACLE AVOIDANCE

- If you're concerned about germs, give that porker a peck on the forehead rather than a kiss on the snout.
- Enlist the aid of a handler to make sure the animal doesn't bolt when asked to perform in front of squealing children.

SUCCESS SNAPSHOTS

- When students dove into their reading at Jacksonville, Florida's Twin Lakes Academy Elementary, Principal Barbara Langley kept a date with a crustacean at a year-end assembly with a "Treasures of the Deep" theme. In an auditorium decked out with plastic palm trees and fish, and surrounded by students and staffers in tropical duds, Langley dyed her hair purple and red to mimic a sea anemone. She then planted two salty kisses on a live lobster, the *Florida Times-Union* reported. Before completing her stunt, she tried to get away with smooching a plastic lobster, but Assistant Principal Alan Due objected, saying, "That isn't fair. That lobster isn't alive." After really making good on her promise while students cheered, Langley said, "This is what happens when you reach your goals. You have a good time. I am so proud of you" (Scanlan, 2003).

- Assistant Principal Freda Malphurs knew she had to top Principal Ginny Yanson's kiss of a pig named Puddin' Pie that rewarded students at Wesley Chapel, Florida's Quail Hollow Elementary for hitting a 25,000-book reading goal. After all, the students had read nearly 38,000 books to meet the next year's challenge. So Malphurs agreed to kiss Sally the Burmese python—at three separate assemblies. The administrator did cheat a bit, planting a peck atop the head of the 20-foot, 200-pound snake as a dozen teachers held it up. But the screaming students didn't seem to mind. "It wasn't slimy or anything. It was pretty smooth," Malphurs told the *Tampa Tribune*. "So it wasn't really that bad" (Jewell, 1998).

- When the 544 students at West Chester, Pennsylvania's Glen Acres Elementary plowed through 2,000 books in just six weeks one fall, Principal Susan Huber rewarded them by kissing a Guernsey cow at an all-school New Year's celebration. Before Huber entered on a motorcycle, though, students had to read for an additional 2,000 seconds each—or just over 33 minutes. In the weeks before the celebration, kids had their parents sign cards sporting the title of each book they completed. A chart on prominent display in the school tracked overall progress. Every class also collected 2,000 pennies during the challenge period, with the $600 total earmarked for children's cancer research. "You saw kids reading in their spare time and would hear them asking each other in the halls about what book they were reading now," Huber told the *Philadelphia Inquirer.* One pleased parent said the stunt "kept the kids focused during the holidays, which is hard. They wanted to read as much as possible and then read some more" (Fine, 2000).

- Principal Kristin Berryman issued a two-tiered challenge to the 800 students at Newman, Georgia's White Oak Elementary: Read 2,000 books and she'd kiss a pig; but read 4,000, and she'd smooch a frog, too. After the pupils devoured nearly 4,000 texts, Berryman kept her end of the deal and puckered up to a 300-pound pig named Charlotte. In the weeks leading up to the kiss, Berryman modeled various shades of lipstick during the school's closed-circuit TV broadcasts to students. Even though they didn't quite meet both challenges, "I don't know of a student that didn't read one or two books to help me get to that goal," Berryman told the *Atlanta Journal-Constitution*. "A lot of our kids gave up their recess. That's how motivated they were" (Carter, 2002).

CURRICULUM RESOURCES

Critters with character lesson plans. (2003) Washington, DC: Humane Society Press.

No. 14: Human Sundae

Silliness Rating: 5
Gross-Out Rating: 4
Mix-and-Match Possibilities: Stunt No. 100

Basic Stunt: Let students dress you up as an ice-cream sundae

FRILLS, CHILLS, & SPILLS

- Host an ice-cream social with real sundaes to cap off the celebration.
- Give the top scoring student the honor of planting the cherry atop your head at the end of the stunt.

LEARNING LINKS

- From *gelato* to flavored snow, explore the different icy treats enjoyed around the world in a social studies unit.
- Adapt math activities to the stunt, challenging students to figure out how many sprinkles it will take to cover you from head to toe, and so on.

OBSTACLE AVOIDANCE

- With nut allergies an increasing concern in schools, it's probably best to stick with candy sprinkles instead.
- Wear clothes you won't mind throwing away after you get hosed down.

SUCCESS SNAPSHOT

- After students at Riverside, California's Val Verde Elementary enlisted a record number of parents into the school's PTA chapter, Principal Jan Marshall let kids cover her in ice cream, sprinkles, cherries, and whipped cream at an assembly open to the entire school community. In addition to the 900-member student body, the audience included several delighted moms and dads, the *Riverside Press-Enterprise* reported (Fetbrandt, 1996).

CURRICULUM RESOURCES

Older, J. (2001). *Ice cream: Great moments in ice cream history.* Watertown, MA: Charlesbridge Publishing.

No. 15: Get In-Line

Silliness Rating: 4
Gross-Out Rating: 1
Mix-and-Match Possibilities: Stunts Nos. 4, 7, 8, 12, 18, 22, 29, 49

Basic Stunt: Strap on a pair of skates and roll through the halls

FRILLS, CHILLS, & SPILLS

- Enlist the P.E. teacher to create a fitness unit using skates.
- Celebrate students' academic achievements at a local skating rink.
- Practice some fancy dance moves and jumps to try out in the halls.

LEARNING LINKS

- Ask math students to estimate how many miles you'll skate in the course of a day, how many calories you'll burn, and so on.

OBSTACLE AVOIDANCE

- Pulling off this stunt without pulling a leg muscle will require proper stretching and at least a few practice sessions.

SUCCESS SNAPSHOT

- The citizens of Cranston, Rhode Island, got a glimpse of a dedicated educator in action when Horton Elementary Principal Susan DeMay in-line skated all the way across town after her students exceeded their reading goal. DeMay, former goalie for a local hockey team, even wore her old mask on the trek. Students greeted their principal with cheers and supportive signs when she arrived at school. "I did it all for you," DeMay told the children. "What I did is nothing compared to what you did. You are the ones who should be applauded." She later told the *Providence Journal-Bulletin*, "I'm no-nonsense as a principal . . . but you have to have a sense of humor" (Arsenault, 2000).

CURRICULUM RESOURCES

Powell, M., & Svensson, J. (1998). *In-line skating* (2nd ed.). Champaign, IL: Human Kinetics.

No. 16: Karaoke Kings and Queens

Silliness Rating: 4
Gross-Out Rating: 1
Mix-and-Match Possibilities: Stunts Nos. 65, 88

Basic Stunt: Sing along to your favorite hits just like Joan Cusack did as the principal in *School of Rock*

FRILLS, CHILLS, & SPILLS

- Enlist faculty and staff members to form an air-guitar band and back up your act. If possible, dress the part of the pop star whose song you'll be singing.

LEARNING LINKS

- Ask the school choir or a group of music students to work up a real number they can perform as a follow-up to your silly stunt.

OBSTACLE AVOIDANCE

- Vet the lyrics before belting them out to make sure they don't include any words or images inappropriate for young children.

SUCCESS SNAPSHOT

- Karaoke was on tap at the cafeteria of Port St. Lucie, Florida's Port St. Lucie Elementary after students earned an overall A grade on the Florida Comprehensive Assessment Test, up from a C the year before. The celebration included a hamburger and hot-dog barbecue hosted by the PTO and school advisory council, while students decorated the walls with artistic interpretations of the letter A, the *Palm Beach Post* reported. After the singing and eating, the children plastered a smiling Principal Carmen Peterson with a chocolate cream pie ("School celebrates . . . ," 2003).

No. 17: Dance Fever

Silliness Rating: 5
Gross-Out Rating: 1
Mix-and-Match Possibilities: Stunts Nos. 29, 65

Basic Stunt: Host a backwards prom, or "morp," and cut a rug in front of the student body

FRILLS, CHILLS, & SPILLS

- Surprise students with a silly, but highly choreographed, dance routine.

LEARNING LINKS

- Ask the P.E. staff to incorporate dance moves into student fitness routines.

OBSTACLE AVOIDANCE

- Make sure to stretch properly before strutting your stuff on the dance floor.

SUCCESS SNAPSHOT

- After a service-learning project raised $5,000 to sponsor a child through the Make-A-Wish Foundation, students at Schilling Farms Middle School in Collierville, Tennessee, celebrated with a "morp" dance—a parody of a traditional prom. The kids dressed in T-shirts and jeans for the shindig, which also featured wacky moves from several faculty members. Students earlier had voted with pennies to decide which teachers would compete in a dance contest. History instructor Bill Finley took the top prize by incorporating calisthenics into his routine. "When you have students that are that motivated, we have to support them," school librarian Barbara Jenkins told the *Memphis Commercial Appeal* (Hanna, 2004).

No. 18: Cross-Dressing Camp

Silliness Rating: 4
Gross-Out Rating: 2
Mix-and-Match Possibilities: Stunts Nos. 4, 11, 94

Basic Stunt: Dress up like a member of the opposite sex, following in the high-heeled footsteps of comics ranging from America's Milton Berle to Britain's Monty Python troupe and Canada's Kids in the Hall

FRILLS, CHILLS, & SPILLS

- Adopt a new voice and persona to go with your cross-dressing look.

LEARNING LINKS

- Solicit costume ideas from students in theater and art classes.
- Focus a language-arts and history lesson on the Elizabethan practice of having men play even women's roles in theatrical productions. The discussion can serve as a fun springboard into a Shakespeare unit.

OBSTACLE AVOIDANCE

- Gentle parodies are fine, but avoid offensive gender stereotypes.

SUCCESS SNAPSHOTS

- Spurred on by the promise of a memorable performance by counselor Alex Bacos, students at L.A.'s Madison Middle School raised their scores on California's Stanford 9 tests by a whopping 66 points in one year. So Bacos treated the 2,400 pupils to a rendition of the theme from *The Little Mermaid* while dressed as the film's title character. Splayed in front of an ocean backdrop on the auditorium stage, the counselor sang while showing off his long red wig, gold sequined skirt, shell halter-top, and green swim fins. After his rendition brought down the house, Bacos exclaimed, "You're just clapping because I'm so pretty." Because the school had been labeled underperforming by the state, Bacos told the *L.A. Times,* "We knew that this was a make-or-break year. We had to show improvement." His promised stunt became the motivational centerpiece of a campaign that included extensive parent outreach and Saturday tutoring sessions (Haynes, 2002).
- It was natural for Durham, North Carolina's Hope Valley Elementary and Southwest Elementary to have a friendly reading competition. After all, Hope Valley Principal Betsy Knott is married to Southwest Principal David Sneed. So when students answered the challenge to read 20,000 books, Knott and Sneed made the rounds of both schools dressed as each other. "We will do anything it takes to get children excited," Knott told the *Raleigh News and Observer.* "It shows them that it's important to me that they read—and I'm willing to act silly to get them to read a lot of books" (Goldstein, 2000).

No. 19: The Silent Treatment

Silliness Rating: 2
Gross-Out Rating: 1
Mix-and-Match Possibilities: Stunt No. 89

Basic Stunt: Exercise your right to remain silent for an entire school day

FRILLS, CHILLS, & SPILLS

- Develop a pantomime routine to perform for students during your quiet time.
- Work up a few comedy bits in which members of the faculty and staff try various ploys to get you talking.
- Start the no-talking day in the library, which welcomes quiet patrons.

LEARNING LINKS

- Focus a theater unit on the art of the mime.
- Devote part of the language-arts program to teaching sign language.

OBSTACLE AVOIDANCE

- Tell regular callers in advance why you won't be available to talk during your day of silence.

SUCCESS SNAPSHOT

- After years of motivating students by reclining into containers of rotten eggs and communing with dozens of snakes, Principal Alan Cook of Orangevale, California's Green Oaks Fundamental School said, "We thought we'd do something that wasn't in the 'gross' category." So he promised to spend a day with his lips sealed if students met their annual reading goal. To prepare for the big day, Cook took mime lessons. Even with that training, staying silent proved a challenge for the administrator. "I'm kind of famous for my talking ability—I'm rather verbal," he said. But Cook expressed optimism that he'd pull off the stunt with style. "We always end these things with a huge assembly. Usually the kids write songs and poems about the stunt. All of the kids come, as do many of the parents. So this will end with a big show where I have to get up and do something in mime."

SOURCE: Telephone interview with Alan Cook, August 27, 2002.

CURRICULUM RESOURCES

Kipnis, C. (1990). *The mime book.* Colorado Springs, CO: Meriwhether Publishing.
Flodin, M. (1991). *Signing for kids.* New York: Perigee.
Flodin, M. (1994). *Signing illustrated: The complete learning guide.* New York: Perigee.
Flodin, M. (1995). *Signing is fun: A child's introduction to the basics of sign language.* New York: Perigee.

No. 20: Duct Tape Delights

Silliness Rating: 5
Gross-Out Rating: 1
Mix-and-Match Possibilities: Stunts Nos. 22, 94

Basic Stunt: Allow students to duct-tape you to a wall

FRILLS, CHILLS, & SPILLS

- Stick the stunt in the minds of students by showing up at school in a duct-tape tuxedo. (At least consider donning a duct-tape tie.)

LEARNING LINKS

- Encourage children to try their hand at duct-tape craft projects in art class.
- Ask students to calculate how much tape it will take to hold your weight to the wall.

OBSTACLE AVOIDANCE

- If you're worried the tape won't hold you, try the trick employed by one principal—screw small wooden footholds into the wall to help carry the load.

SUCCESS SNAPSHOT

- After Principal Chris Dunning promised students at New Port Richey, Florida's Calusa Elementary that they could duct tape him to the cafeteria wall if they read 60,000 pages in three weeks, they plowed through a remarkable 122,657 pages. So, as promised, Dunning literally hung around the lunchroom for several hours, held up by several rolls of tape. "The kids have been working hard for this," he told the *Tampa Tribune*. "It's been the best reading incentive we've done" (Blair, 2002).

CURRICULUM RESOURCES

Berg, J., Nyberg, T., & Dierckins, T. (2000). *The jumbo duct tape book.* New York: Workman.

Schiedermayer, E. (2002). *Got tape?: Roll out the fun with duct tape.* Iola, WI: Krause Publications.

Wilson, J. (1999). *Ductigami: The art of the tape.* Erin, ONT: Boston Mills Press.

No. 21: Up, Up, and Away

Silliness Rating: 2
Gross-Out Rating: 1
Mix-and-Match Possibilities: Stunts Nos. 7, 10

Basic Stunt: Soar over your school in a hot-air balloon

FRILLS, CHILLS, & SPILLS

- Can't find a balloon? Other principals have motivated students to learn by flying over their schools in helicopters and even crop dusters.

LEARNING LINKS

- The sky's the limit when it comes to lessons that can be linked to the history and science of flight.

OBSTACLE AVOIDANCE

- Use a professional flight service with a strong safety record and up-to-date liability insurance.
- Resist the temptation to let students hop aboard unless their parents have signed liability waivers.

SUCCESS SNAPSHOTS

- A few weeks before the end of the school year, Principal Elizabeth Roscoe saw that her students at Hampton, Virginia's Tucker-Capps Elementary were short of their 40,000-book reading goal. "Guess I won't have to do it after all," she told them, referring to her promised celebratory stunt. Spurred on by this gentle teasing, the children ended the year with 40,934 books to their credit, the *Newport News Daily Press* reported. So Roscoe set aside her fear of heights and took a spin in a hot-air balloon. Dressed in 1890s costumes, Roscoe and reading specialist Christine Gergely entered the playground on the back of a Corvette, then climbed aboard the green-and-black balloon, which soon rose 60 feet above the delighted students. And guess which song played over the PA system? Why, "Up, Up and Away," of course (Tan, 1998).
- It was a lofty goal for the 200 students of Shreveport, Louisiana's Barret Elementary: Read 8,000 books over the course of the year. But with Principal John Kerley promising to take off in a hot-air balloon, the children read almost 12,000 books. The number of students scoring at an unsatisfactory level on the state's LEAP 21 test also dropped by some 65 percent. On the big day, Kerley and the pilot explained to the students how the balloon stays aloft. And then they took off for a short flight. Why take to the air? "Reading is the foundation for all backgrounds," Kerley told the *Shreveport Times*. "If a child can't read, he or she won't do well in math or science" (Hughes, 2000).

CURRICULUM RESOURCES

Carson, M. K. (2003). *The Wright Brothers for kids: How they invented the airplane—21 activities exploring the science and history of flight.* Chicago: Chicago Review Press.

No. 22: Superheroic Stunts

Silliness Rating: 4
Gross-Out Rating: 1
Mix-and-Match Possibilities: Stunts Nos. 12, 15, 25, 27, 51, 59, 60, 69, 72

Basic Stunt: Transform yourself from mild-mannered educator into superhero for a day

FRILLS, CHILLS, & SPILLS

- Rig a pulley system inside the gymnasium that will hoist you high above a cheering crowd of students.

LEARNING LINKS

- How can a superhero stunt tie into the curriculum and give your science instruction a bionic boost? I asked University of Minnesota physics professor James Kakalios, who teaches a freshman course called Science in Comic Books, for a few pointers that would translate well into high school classrooms. Noting that many comic-book heroes—including the Flash, the Atom, Batman, the Fantastic Four's Mr. Fantastic, and Professor X of the X-Men are also scientists—Kakalios happily obliged.

  Paradoxically, effective superhero science units must start by accepting that the costumed crusaders actually possess their scientifically impossible powers. But then you can analyze whether the feats the heroes perform using those powers actually follow the laws of physics. "Once you buy into the super power you ask, 'Is the rest plausible or not?'" Kakalios explains, using the example of the lightning-fast Flash. "For instance, could you run up the side of a building? Yes. Could you run across the ocean? Yes. Could you drag people along in your wake? Yes. And we analyze this. We talk about the Bernoulli principle that would come into play. We talk about what escape velocities are."

  One popular example in the class focuses on a pivotal event in the Spider-Man series. "We talk about a storyline that happened in Spider-Man, the death of Gwen Stacey," the professor says. "There's a story where Spider-Man's girlfriend gets knocked off a bridge by the Green Goblin, and Spider-Man catches her in his webbing at the last possible second, yet discovers that she's dead. I've given this as a problem in my introductory physics classes. You fall off a bridge 300 feet high. How fast are you going near the base? You're going nearly 95 mph. And then you ask, If you have half of a second to stop someone, and they have to go from 95 mph to zero, how much force do you have to supply? The answer is, about 10 Gs—ten times gravity. So it's not at all surprising that she died. And then you make the point that this is why we have airbags in our cars. Because when you're going 60 miles per hour and your car stops, you're still moving at 60, and something's got to stop your head. If it's the steering column, the time available is very short and the force is very high. Airbags, because they deform under pressure, maintain contact longer. They have more time available to slow you down, so the force they have to supply is less."

So who's the best character to use in a superhero science unit? "If I had to pick just one, I would say the Flash," Kakalios says. "That would simply be because, as you change velocity, by using the Flash you could introduce issues of conservation of energy. And at different speeds, different phenomena come into effect. We can talk about Doppler shifts. We can talk about the sound barriers. We can even get into relativistic effects, when he's moving near light speed."

Counterintuitively, using these heroic fantasy figures to teach science "promotes the whole notion that the world is a knowable place," Kakalios contends. "You can get the students to eat their spinach if you hide it in this ice-cream sundae."

OBSTACLE AVOIDANCE

- Keep your super ear to the ground to discover which costumed crusaders are most popular with your students. Today's youngsters might be more thrilled by a visit from SpongeBob SquarePants than Wonder Woman, for instance.

SUCCESS SNAPSHOTS

- Using stunts to promote reading, James Reed, principal of John Ireland Elementary in Dallas, has done everything from moving his office to the school roof to dashing around the grounds on horseback. But when Reed simply dressed up as Batman, the kids loved it just as much. "Kids enjoy entertainment, and they are obsessed with television," he told the *Dallas Morning News.* "If we can take some of those characters and move them into the school, it can really motivate the kids" (Gillman, 2000).

- When students at Clover, South Carolina's Griggs Road Elementary excelled in an extracurricular math program, Principal Paul Pratt showed up at school dressed as Batman. Another year, he portrayed nerdy Steve Urkel from the classic ABC sitcom *Family Matters.* "It's important for kids to see principals in this light sometimes and not see the principal as the guy who sits in an office behind a door," Pratt told the *Charlotte Observer.* He believes it takes a creative approach to pull children away from video games and the Internet. "We can't compete with these things unless we make education really exciting and fun for these kids," Pratt said. "If I need to dress up and make a fool out of myself, I'll do it" (Goldstein, 2000).

CURRICULUM RESOURCES

Weiner, S. (2003). *The 101 best graphic novels.* New York: NBM Publishing.

No. 23: In the Swim

Silliness Rating: 4
Gross-Out Rating: 2
Mix-and-Match Possibilities: Stunts Nos. 67, 85

Basic Stunt: Go jump in a lake—or even the ocean

FRILLS, CHILLS, & SPILLS

- Heighten the thrill by taking a "polar bear" swim during the coldest month of the year.

LEARNING LINKS

- This stunt ties in well with natural science units on aquatic life, and can be the centerpiece of a yearlong ocean theme.

OBSTACLE AVOIDANCE

- Make sure you've got a strong swimmer for a spotter, preferably someone who knows CPR.

SUCCESS SNAPSHOT

- Principal Jenda Turner twice swam across a duck pond on the campus of San Juan Capistrano, California's Rancho Capistrano Christian School after students exceeded a fundraising goal. She wore a wetsuit and snorkeling gear for the stunt, and made sure not to swallow any of the brackish water. "I walked out with the wetsuit on," the principal recalls. "I didn't just pop out of my car and into the lake. I put on the full show." Turner only planned to swim the pond once, but one class arrived late, so she repeated the aquatic performance. The best thing about the stunt from the principal's perspective is how it inspired even the older children at the preK–8 school. "It's difficult to get the middle school students excited about things," Turner notes. "Elementary's always excited, but the middle school students were just ecstatic to see their principal do this. You must seem larger than life to them sometimes, and I think in their minds to see you kind of come down to their level and just have a goofy fun time is kind of cool, and even meaningful to them."

SOURCE: Telephone interview with Jenda Turner, September 26, 2003.

No. 24: Saddle Up

Silliness Rating: 3
Gross-Out Rating: 1
Mix-and-Match Possibilities: Stunts Nos. 29, 42, 81

Basic Stunt: Prance around the school on the back of a horse or mule

FRILLS, CHILLS, & SPILLS

- Dress up as a knight and call yourself Sir-Reads-a-Lot, as several principals have done to encourage students to hoof their way into the library.

LEARNING LINKS

- Tie the stunt into a yearlong learning theme focused on farm life, or at least harness it to a natural science unit on horses.

OBSTACLE AVOIDANCE

- Keep students far enough away so they don't get kicked—or spook the horse and send you flying. Calm, older horses work best for these types of stunts.

SUCCESS SNAPSHOT

- Not nearly as comfortable in the saddle as he is in the principal's office, Bob Potter still attempted to treat his students at Sugar City, Idaho's Central Elementary to a display of trick riding after they exceeded their reading goal. Potter, dressed as Sir Reads-a-Lot, soon got thrown. But he simply dusted himself off and read the following proclamation: "Be it hereby known now and forever that students at Central Elementary in Sugar City, Idaho, have read in excess of 31,000 books, to assure the fact that they know how to have a good time and are exceptionally smart." The knight-educator then challenged the children to races—but on broomstick horses this time. Potter's previous stunts included leaping into a vat of macaroni and cheese. "I'm not a horse guy," Potter told the *Idaho Falls Post Register*. "I'd almost prefer the hot macaroni. Almost, but not quite" (Davidson, 2001).

No. 25: The Mysterious Reader

Silliness Rating: 3
Gross-Out Rating: 1
Mix-and-Match Possibilities: Stunts Nos. 3, 22, 29, 49

Basic Stunt: Promote literacy with a "mystery reader" program that brings in fascinating guest storytellers

FRILLS, CHILLS, & SPILLS

- Many schools enlist teachers, parents, and other community members to make guest storytelling appearances as classroom mystery readers during Children's Book Week in November. When readers come from outside of school, students play a version of "What's My Line?"—asking questions until they discover who the guests are and what they do for a living. So the sessions provide interesting previews of adult life in addition to involving parents and other community members in the classroom. As one program coordinator put it, "Mystery Reader provides a new face for the second-graders and gives them, at an early age, ideas about career possibilities. And the program reinforces the importance of knowing how to read and write to be successful in life."
- At some schools, mystery readers show up in disguises or hide behind screens—especially teachers and administrators the children might easily recognize otherwise.
- In *School Wide Book Events,* author Virginia Lawrence Ray offers a fun twist on the concept (Ray, 2003). Start by encouraging students to keep an eye out for mystery readers throughout the school day, she suggests. Then, enlist teachers, parents, administrators, and other volunteers to don a designated mysterious costume—Ray recommends a colorful vest festooned with feathers and sequins—and read in an open area of the school for 10 minutes or so. When students spot the mystery reader, they can fill out sighting forms and then drop them into boxes by grade level to be entered in a drawing for free books.

LEARNING LINKS

- In addition to promoting literacy, mystery reader programs help students hone their critical-thinking skills as they work to uncover the identities of their guests.

OBSTACLE AVOIDANCE

- When bringing in volunteers from the community, make sure to issue basic costume guidelines and sign off on their story choices in advance.

SUCCESS SNAPSHOTS

- A day of guest mystery readers capped off a monthlong Reading Jamboree at Poe Elementary in Arlington Heights, Illinois. After starting the month with a celebratory assembly, the school held book swaps that allowed students to trade in books from home for new ones they wanted to read. Next came a popcorn party with the acronym DEAR—for "drop everything and read"—and a "poetry jam" where students performed original verse or favorite poems. More than 30 mystery readers showed up from the community to end the jamboree with a bang. Why all the hoopla? "It's to celebrate the successes that students have had throughout the year in reading," Principal Pam Lindberg told the *Chicago Daily Herald* (Cutrer, 2002).

- As part of a monthlong "Get Clued into Reading" campaign, students at Vista, New York's Meadow Pond Elementary enjoyed a series of mystery readers who seemed familiar—probably because they were parents dressed up in silly costumes. Children who met their reading goals received keys that unlocked a treasure chest stocked with good books. They also got to participate in a schoolwide treasure hunt. "Kids really get into it; they love it," Librarian Kathy Lauterbach told the *Westchester County Journal News* (Kelley, 2004).

CURRICULUM RESOURCES

Ray, V. L. (2003). *School wide book events: How to make them happen.* Westport, CT: Libraries Unlimited.

No. 26: Dye Laughing

Silliness Rating: 4
Gross-Out Rating: 1
Mix-and-Match Possibilities: Stunts Nos. 1, 100

Basic Stunt: Get a crazy dye job in front of the student body

FRILLS, CHILLS, & SPILLS

- If you promise to dye your hair some garish color, consider teasing the students a bit by coming out wearing a clown wig in that color.

When the hooting and hollering subsides, take off the wig to reveal your real dyed locks.

- Give students votes based on the number of pages or books read and allow them to select one of several silly hairstyles or colors you will have to endure. Alternately, let them vote on which member of the faculty or staff will have to join you in getting a dye job.

LEARNING LINKS

- Ask students to give you a virtual makeover in art class.

OBSTACLE AVOIDANCE

- Follow the "strand test" on the dye box to make sure you're not allergic to the coloring.
- Dye your hair in a well-ventilated area and be careful not to get any of the goop in your eyes.
- Choose a "semi-permanent" variety if you want to wash that dye right out of your hair.
- Wear a shirt you can live without in case there's spillage.

SUCCESS SNAPSHOTS

- After students at Santa Ana, California's McFadden Intermediate zoomed through 2 million pages to hit their annual reading goal, Principal Esther Severy went from blonde hair to pink and added 50 spikes. "I would ride a donkey, sit on the roof or, if they had an elephant, I would ride that—anything that was reasonable that wouldn't hurt me or hurt anyone else," Severy told the *Orange County Register.* "I was embarrassed to go on duty out front at the end of the day. Yeah, it's a gimmick. But if in the end kids read more than they would have, then it's worth it." Parents confirmed that the promise of a stunt spurred their children to read more books (Radcliffe, 2003).
- When students at Burlington, Iowa's Blackhawk Elementary raised enough money to buy 16 acres of Belize rainforest, Principal Karen Waldorf celebrated their service-learning success by dyeing her hair a different color every day for a week. She started with silver on Monday, then segued into blue, purple, pink, and green. "I'm glad I didn't say I would spray it a different color for every acre they adopted," Waldorf told the *Burlington Hawk Eye.* "They did a wonderful job meeting this challenge" (Cleland, 2000).

No. 27: Bungee Banzai!

Silliness Rating: 3
Gross-Out Rating: 1
Mix-and-Match Possibilities: Stunts Nos. 22, 100

Basic Stunt: Hang out in front of the school by your ankle after jumping off a bungee platform

FRILLS, CHILLS, & SPILLS

- Agree to wear a blindfold during the stunt if students exceed their educational goal by a set amount.

LEARNING LINKS

- Use this stunt to illustrate physics principles in an entertaining way.

OBSTACLE AVOIDANCE

- Investigate the safety record of the amusement company operating the bungee ride, and check the equipment thoroughly before strapping yourself in.

SUCCESS SNAPSHOTS

- Now a superintendent in Palm Beach County, Florida, Art Johnson is legendary in his community for the motivational stunts he used to pull off as a principal. One year, he bungee-jumped from the ceiling of the gymnasium. In an even more daring effort, he once plunged two stories into a kiddie pool containing only four inches of water—and he was wearing a tuxedo at the time. Through it all, Johnson never took his leadership potential for granted. "You can take a poor school and put a good principal in and that school will turn around overnight," he told the *Fort Lauderdale Sun-Sentinel* (Solomon, 2003).
- Barry Riehle is known for teaching one of the toughest courses at Anderson Township, Ohio's Turpin High. But students flock to his

AP physics course anyway, in part because he finds such entertaining ways to impart knowledge and spur academic achievement. For instance, Riehle once illustrated a lesson on gravity by bungee jumping with a gravity meter tied to his back. "What I really like to do is turn on lights inside other people's heads," he told the *Cincinnati Enquirer*. "The second component is, I don't like to be bored. The third component is, I'm a ham" (Kranz, 2004).

No. 28: Slime Time

Silliness Rating: 5
Gross-Out Rating: 5
Mix-and-Match Possibilities: Stunts Nos. 8, 100

Basic Stunt: Let students cover you in radioactive-green "slime"

FRILLS, CHILLS, & SPILLS

- In a very real sense, the Nickelodeon children's cable TV network was built on a slippery mountain of colorful "slime." The goopy, gloppy substance has been such an enduring feature of Nickelodeon shows that a splat of slime rests under the network's logo. Stars as big as Jim Carrey have been covered with the stuff at the channel's annual Kids' Choice Awards. ("It feels like love, man, slimy-gooey love," the comedian said after being doused.) But what is slime, and how can you make your own batch? "Slime is a naturally occurring substance that we get from our slime geyser at Nickelodeon Studios Florida," Dave Aizer, host of a program called *Slimetime LIVE*, confided during a chat session on the Nickelodeon Web site. Maybe so, but shows such as *You Can't Do That on Television* and *Double Dare* used some of the following recipes to make their slime. Any one of these should work just fine for your purposes as well.

Smooth Slime

Ingredients: Vanilla pudding mix, milk, corn syrup, green food coloring.

Directions: Follow pudding instructions, but add extra milk. Mix in syrup and food coloring.

Chunky Slime

Ingredients: Cottage cheese, milk, green food coloring.

Directions: Mix and pour.

No-More-Tears Slime

Ingredients: Oats, water, green food coloring, baby shampoo.

Directions: Mix the first three ingredients, and then slowly stir in the shampoo to keep the slime from sudsing up.

Super Slime

Ingredients: Cream of Wheat, water, baby shampoo, green food coloring

Directions: Mix and pour—with or without an optional dollop of liquid latex.

LEARNING LINKS

- Employ slime in messy, volcanic, and entertainingly educational science experiments.

OBSTACLE AVOIDANCE

- Bring a change of clothes—and be prepared to discard the ones that get slimed.
- No matter how tempting it seems, please refrain from eating the slime dripping down your face.

SUCCESS SNAPSHOT

- Principal Vickie Violette took a dip in an inflatable pool filled with slime—which consisted of green Jell-O, gummy worms, and spaghetti—to celebrate the fundraising prowess of students at Knoxville, Tennessee's Adrian Burnett Elementary. Teachers incorporated the slime stunt into reading, writing, and math units before returning to more traditional lessons. "We tried to turn it into learning activities," Violette told the *Knoxville News-Sentinel*. "And when the slime is done, it's done. We are going to settle down after this" (Lawson, 2003).

CURRICULUM RESOURCES

Green, J. (2000). *The mad scientist handbook: The do-it-yourself guide to making your own rock candy, anti-gravity machine, edible glass, rubber eggs, fake blood, green slime, and much much more.* New York: Perigee.

Marks, D. F. (2003). *Glues, brews, and goos: Recipes and formulas for almost any classroom project* (Vol. 2, 2nd ed.). Westport, CT: Libraries Unlimited.

Wellnitz, W. R. (1993). *Homemade slime and rubber bones!: Awesome science activities.* New York: McGraw-Hill.

No. 29: What a Character!

Silliness Rating: 5
Gross-Out Rating: 1
Mix-and-Match Possibilities: Stunts Nos. 64, 94

Basic Stunt: Dress up as a gorilla or other goofy character and go ape in front of students

FRILLS, CHILLS, & SPILLS

- Promise to take the stunt to a higher level if students surpass their goals. For instance, if you dress up as a great ape, climb into the gymnasium rafters and toss down bananas when the children exceed expectations.

LEARNING LINKS

- Add a strong educational component by portraying important historical figures that dovetail with your state's social studies standards instead.

OBSTACLE AVOIDANCE

- Gorilla costumes heat up quickly. Drink plenty of fluids and take frequent breaks to avoid heat stroke.

SUCCESS SNAPSHOTS

- After scaling the 25-foot bell tower at Rancho Santa Margarita, California's Melinda Heights Elementary, Principal Don Snyder climbed into an ape suit and tossed bananas down to bemused students celebrating the attainment of a PTA fundraising goal. "It's OK to be goofy," Snyder told the *Orange County Register.* However, he added, "You don't want a situation where a student has a malicious attitude toward an adult" (Radcliffe, 2003).

- He might not be a man of a thousand faces, but Principal Mack Mitchell did manage to impersonate a handful of famous figures from U.S. history after each student at Edmond, Oklahoma's Russell Dougherty Elementary read 10 books in the first month of school. Dressed as Paul Revere, Mitchell rode a horse past the school. Later, he sang patriotic tunes gussied up as the Statue of Liberty. He also portrayed a pilgrim and Abraham Lincoln during the daylong reading fest that capped off the challenge. "I wanted to do something wacky, but not life threatening," Mitchell told the *Daily Oklahoman* (Killackey, 1992).

- It's hard enough to ride a unicycle without having to keep your balance in an ape suit. That's probably why Principal Sam Foust didn't pedal very far at Brown Summit, North Carolina's Monticello-Brown Summit Elementary before he fell over in front of a cheering student body. Foust performed the stunt, and then posed for dozens of pictures, after the children hit an Accelerated Reader goal. By the end of the assembly, he probably wished he had just dressed up like Elvis, as he had the previous year. Dressed as an ape on an 82-degree day, "It was as hot as it could be inside that costume," Foust told the *Greensboro News & Record.* "It just about killed me" (Newsom, 1998b).

- As part of the guest reader program at Alamo, California's Rancho Romero Elementary, Principal Marilyn McCurdy invited a third-grade class to give her a costume makeover after she read *Principal's New Clothes,* an update of Hans Christian Andersen's classic *The Emperor's New Clothes.* Wearing layers of long underwear, McCurdy let students turn her into a giant dress-up doll, outfitting her with crazy chapeaux, silly scarves, tutus, sweaters, and skirts. "Every week here we have a mystery reader come in and read," the principal told the *Tri-Valley Herald.* "This week I was their reader. You have to stand outside the door and talk in a funny voice, and they have to guess who you are. It's really fun" (Benca, 2003).

CURRICULUM RESOURCES

Calmenson, S. (1991). *Principal's new clothes.* New York: Scholastic.

No. 30: Camping on Campus

Silliness Rating: 4
Gross-Out Rating: 1
Mix-and-Match Possibilities: Stunts Nos. 10, 66, 83

Basic Stunt: Set up a tent and host a sleepover at school

FRILLS, CHILLS, & SPILLS

- At one school, the music teacher wrote and performed a parody version of the Drifters' "Up on the Roof" to commemorate her principal's camping excursion atop the school.

LEARNING LINKS

- Adopt a "great outdoors" theme for the school year that culminates with this stunt.
- Tie in a service-learning unit on homelessness that encourages students to help less-fortunate members of your community.

OBSTACLE AVOIDANCE

- Dress warmly, and make sure the security staff knows about your overnight stay.

SUCCESS SNAPSHOTS

- Principal George MacKay had so little camping experience, he had to buy a new tent for his night on the roof of Virginia Beach, Virginia's College Park Elementary. He was glad to rough it, though, after students increased the school's PTA membership to 80 percent of parents, up from just 53 percent a year earlier. In the weeks before the event, every student who enlisted a member was allowed to sign the blue pajamas MacKay would wear—along with fake-fur animal foot slippers. The children and their parents helped him pass the time by holding a "Hamburgers and Homework" event on the school grounds, the *Virginian-Pilot* reported (Young, 1999).

- A first-time camper, Principal Michael Silverman used a borrowed tent and sleeping bag when he spent the night atop Philadelphia's Penrose Elementary. After downing a cold cheese sandwich for dinner, at least he was able to catch up on his reading. It was a fitting way to spend the evening, since Silverman was camping to reward students for reaching a reading goal. "It's a great incentive," teacher June Washington told the *Philadelphia Daily News*. Added a parent, "He got them to read, which is important" (Nolan, 1995).

No. 31: The Condiment Caper

Silliness Rating: 5
Gross-Out Rating: 4
Mix-and-Match Possibilities: Stunts Nos. 94, 100

Basic Stunt: Dress up like a hot dog in a cardboard or foam-rubber bun, and allow students to add the fixings

FRILLS, CHILLS, & SPILLS

- If you don't want to look like too much of a hot dog, try a tasty twist on this stunt by letting the kids butter you up as a human PB&J sandwich between two cardboard bread slices.
- Hold an old-fashioned wienie roast in connection with the event, inviting parents and other members of the school community.
- Tie in the theme of your academic challenge to the promised stunt with slogans such as "Read Your Way into the Wiener's Circle," or "Be a Math Hot Dog."

LEARNING LINKS

- Incorporate hot-dog facts into math lessons, and ask kids to calculate how much ketchup and relish they'll need to coat you from top to bottom.

OBSTACLE AVOIDANCE

- Skip the mustard—it stings. And consider wearing goggles.
- Wear clothing you're prepared to throw away after the stunt.

SUCCESS SNAPSHOTS

- Wearing a foam mattress pad for a bun, Principal Linda Hannum hot-dogged her way around the grounds of Temecula, California's Linfield Lower School after her K-5 students read at least 75 minutes per week as part of a Super Quiet Uninterrupted Individual Reading Minutes (SQUIRM) initiative. The gleeful children loaded up their top-dog principal with ketchup, mustard, and relish after the Oscar Meyer Wienermobile stopped by for a visit. "It was worth it to have the kids read so much," Hannum told the *Riverside Press-Enterprise* (Bartholomew, 1993). "It's always fun to keep them motivated. We've actually forced families to have time together. And the benefits have been academic achievement, the love of reading, and having family time."

- After a successful service-learning project at Haines City, Florida's Bethune Academy, Principal Sharon Knowles dressed in a red sweat suit, nestled herself into a custom crafted foam bun, and allowed students to spray her with condiments. There were two ground rules—"be nice" and "not above the neck"—but that didn't stop students from dousing the red-hot principal with ketchup, mustard, mayonnaise, relish, and five pounds of onions. "This morning I woke up envisioning what this was going to be like and thought, 'I can't believe I'm doing this,'" Knowles told the *Lakeland Ledger* (Murphy, 1997).

- After dressing as a hot dog to reward students at Colfax, North Carolina's Colfax Elementary for meeting an Accelerated Reader goal, Principal Linda York had two important pieces of advice for any educator considering such a stunt: Maintain a sense of childlike fun, and skip the mustard. "You have to think like a kid. An adult would think this is humiliation. The kids all think it's just great fun," York told the *Greensboro News & Record,* adding, "I didn't realize that mustard would burn so much" (Newsom, 1998b).

- You don't have to get doused with Dijon to pull off an effective hot-dog stunt. Principal Sandra McGary-Ervin rewarded the academic achievements of students at Mableton, Georgia's Harmony Leland Elementary simply by donning a hot-dog suit and busting a move to "Who Let the Dogs Out?" Another time, she wore a wedding dress and treated the children to a violin solo. "I have no problem doing whatever it takes to motivate children," McGary-Ervin told the *Atlanta Journal-Constitution* (Carter, 2002).

CURRICULUM RESOURCES

Graulich, D. (1999). *The hot dog companion: A connoisseur's guide to the food we love.* New York: Lebhar-Friedman.

No. 32: Pie Fight!

Silliness Rating: 5
Gross-Out Rating: 4
Mix-and-Match Possibilities: Stunts Nos. 8, 44

Basic Stunt: Take a pie in the face to reward
student achievement

FRILLS, CHILLS, & SPILLS

- Give top students the option of either tossing pies or receiving one
  in the kisser. Many children will happily choose a pie in the face.

LEARNING LINKS

- This stunt provides a tasty tie-in to a math unit on *pi*.

OBSTACLE AVOIDANCE

- Consider wearing goggles to keep pie out of your eyes—and watch
  your step on the inevitable mess.

SUCCESS SNAPSHOTS

- When students at Monroeville, Pennsylvania's Evergreen
  Elementary read so many books the titles filled a list long enough to
  wrap around the school, Principal Celine Kandala braved a dozen
  pies in the face. Goggles, a shower cap, and a garbage-bag tunic prepared her well for the barrage. Interestingly, when the eight top
  readers got to choose whether to toss pies or get hit by them, they
  chose the latter option. "The kids respond," Kandala told the
  Pittsburgh Post-Gazette. "I think it's because we add the element of
  fun, and we make the books accessible to the kids" (Chute, 1994).
- Principal Terry Usery and Assistant Principal Beverly Putnam
  added a fun twist to the pie-throwing stunt when they pitted the
  boys against the girls in a reading challenge at Belmont, North
  Carolina's Page Elementary. If the boys won, Putnam was to be

pelted with pie, the *Charlotte Observer* reported. But if the girls were victorious, Usery was facing a face full of whipped cream—which is exactly how the contest ended (Goldstein, 1997).

- Making good on a promise after students at Lynden, Washington's Fisher Elementary reached a reading goal, Principal Brad Jernberg and teacher Ron Hanson tossed pies at each other during an assembly that also celebrated the school's first-place finish in a state science competition, the *Bellingham Herald* reported (Shindruk, 2002).

- Near a banner declaring, "The more you read, the more you succeed," Principal Linda White and Assistant Principal Cecilia Chester poked their heads through holes in a plywood sheet and let students pelt them with pies on the playground of Home Gardens, California's Home Gardens Elementary. The children had far surpassed their leisure reading goals for the year, so the two administrators donned goggles and took their whipped-cream facials in good humor on Reading Celebration Day. "They do math and other things, but reading is every day," reading specialist Cathy Trotter told the *Riverside Press-Enterprise*. "Every child's homework is to read at night" (Acosta, 2001).

No. 33: Everything's Backwards

Silliness Rating: 4
Gross-Out Rating: 1
Mix-and-Match Possibilities: Stunts Nos. 15, 18, 94

Basic Stunt: Declare a backwards day at school

FRILLS, CHILLS, & SPILLS

- Encourage everyone to wear their clothing backwards and inside out. Tell the children good-bye as they arrive and hello when they depart, and reverse the class schedule. Finish the day by reading the morning announcements backwards over the PA system.

LEARNING LINKS

- From countdown activities in math to exploring palindromes and reciting the ABCs backwards, this stunt lends itself to fun tie-ins across the curriculum.

OBSTACLE AVOIDANCE

- If you roam the halls backwards, consider donning some look-behind glasses to avoid getting tripped up.

SUCCESS SNAPSHOTS

- After a grueling week of standardized exams, Grand Forks, North Dakota's Lake Agassiz Elementary held a Test Fest celebration in the gym. In addition to a pie-eating contest, a jazz concert, and a round of silly song singing, members of the faculty and staff wore clothing backwards and inside out. The goofy party was geared to ease the tensions of test week. "It's a major undertaking," Principal George Whalen told the *Grand Forks Herald*. "For first graders, it's the first time they've ever taken a standardized test. For little kids, whenever there are tests, there is stress involved. They all want to do well. Their parents want them to do well" (Tobin, 2004).
- Students at Argos, Indiana's Argos Elementary caught the reading bug during the school's Catch a Dragon by the Tale initiative. For every book they read, a paper brick went up in the hall until an entire castle wall appeared. When students exceeded the program's goals, Principal Ron Leichty kept a promise to come to school with his clothes inside out. In addition to an inside-out suit, he sported a knight's helmet to tie into the theme. Teachers and students all dressed in medieval costumes as well. In addition to fond memories, each student took home a free book from the celebration, the *South Bend Tribune* reported (Chipman, 2002).

CURRICULUM RESOURCES

Williams, L. E. (1998). *Backwards day.* New York: Avon.

No. 34: Good Sports

Silliness Rating: 3
Gross-Out Rating: 1
Mix-and-Match Possibilities: Stunts Nos. 22, 86

Basic Stunt: Challenge a local college or professional sports star to a one-on-one contest

FRILLS, CHILLS, & SPILLS

- Take a leaf from the playbook of legendary gambler Thomas Austin "Amarillo Slim" Preston to tilt the playing field in your favor. That means convincing the star to use unorthodox equipment for the match. For instance, Slim has beat Ping-Pong champions by getting them to play against him using Coke bottles and iron skillets. By practicing with these unlikely "paddles" for weeks in advance of the match, Slim gave himself an edge—and made the matches much more amusing for spectators. He also beat Minnesota Fats at billiards when they both used broomsticks for pool cues, and won a golf match with stuntman Evel Knievel employing a carpenter's hammer for a club (Preston & Dinkin, 2003).

LEARNING LINKS

- A sports-themed stunt offers natural tie-ins to your P.E. program. Sports statistics also lend themselves well to math activities, and many reluctant readers dive into biographies of their favorite sports stars.

OBSTACLE AVOIDANCE

- If you're participating in a contact sport, wear plenty of padding and make sure your professional opponent understands that the competition is just for fun.

SUCCESS SNAPSHOT

- No one challenged him to a tackling contest, but Green Bay Packers offensive lineman Kevin Barry delighted students at Two Rivers, Wisconsin's Koenig Elementary anyway when he visited as a reward for children who met a reading challenge. "If I wouldn't be reading, I wouldn't be where I am today," Barry told the children. As Principal Lisa Quistorf told the *Manitowoc Herald Times Reporter*, "Even a football player has to read. He's been a great lesson" (Weaver, 2004).

CURRICULUM RESOURCES

Farmer, L. S. J. (1999). *Go figure!: Mathematics through sports.* Westport, CT: Teacher Ideas Press.

Preston, T. A., & Dinkin, G. (2003). *Amarillo Slim in a world of fat people: The memoirs of the greatest gambler who ever lived.* New York: HarperCollins.

No. 35: Take a Tumble

Silliness Rating: 4
Gross-Out Rating: 1
Mix-and-Match Possibilities: Stunt No. 91

Basic Stunt: Do a somersault for each book students read

FRILLS, CHILLS, & SPILLS

- If tumbling is too stressful for your weary bones, consider promising to complete one revolution of a jump rope or hula-hoop for each book students read.

LEARNING LINKS

- This stunt ties in perfectly to a fun physical fitness unit in P.E. classes.

OBSTACLE AVOIDANCE

- Consider checking with your doctor before engaging in such strenuous physical activity.

SUCCESS SNAPSHOT

- Principal Rebecca C. W. Adams promised students at Chesapeake, Virginia's Great Bridge Intermediate that she'd turn 1,999 somersaults if they turned 1,999 pages. The children quickly exceeded the goal. "We stopped counting at 3,000 pages," Adams told the *Virginian-Pilot*. "And this year we decided that each student [would] hand in a short summary of each book read. That way, we combined reading skills with writing skills." Meanwhile, the principal set out to keep her end of the bargain by going head over heels down the hallways before moving on to a set of tumbling mats in the gymnasium. By the end of the first day, she had completed 1,000 somersaults in front of various P.E. classes. She completed the second thousand at a 100-tumbles-per-day pace. "I was more weak in the knees than dizzy," Adams said. When her head stopped spinning, the principal set out to complete the second part of her stunt: reading 1,999 pages all by herself during the school year (Feber, 1999).

No. 36: Eggcellent!

Silliness Rating: 5
Gross-Out Rating: 5
Mix-and-Match Possibilities: Stunts Nos. 94, 100

Basic Stunt: Lie down in a bed of rotten eggs

FRILLS, CHILLS, & SPILLS

- Check to see if a local amusement company rents out chicken tic-tac-toe games. If so, take on the chicken in front of the student body before reclining onto all those eggs. Call it *fowl* play, but the chicken almost never loses. That's because the hen gets to play first, and makes subsequent moves on the basis of feed pellets falling into designated slots. The best you can hope for is a draw. I know this because I once ran through many quarters trying to get the best of an addle-brained rooster who kept pecking his way to victory in a tic-tac-toe machine set up at a roadside tourist trap in South Dakota. Even as a child, I was more amused than upset by this losing streak. These days, casinos in Las Vegas, Atlantic City, and Reno regularly set up fancy chicken tic-tac-toe machines to lure customers off the street for a free game. How confident are these casinos that the chicken will beat even the most seasoned gambler? They offer payouts of up to $10,000 to all human winners. That's a lot of chicken scratch, but it usually remains tucked safely inside the casino's henhouse.

LEARNING LINKS

- Tie this stunt into a yearlong "down on the farm" theme. Ask math students to calculate the number of eggs needed to cover you in yolk.

OBSTACLE AVOIDANCE

- Wear clothes you don't mind throwing away.
- Make sure everyone knows that the eggs are past their expiration date, so no one can accuse you of wasting edible food.

SUCCESS SNAPSHOT

- For one of his highly anticipated motivational stunts, Principal Alan Cook of Orangevale, California's Green Oaks Fundamental Elementary lay down in a display case stocked with donated eggs that had passed their expiration dates. First, though, he showed up at school in a horse-drawn cart and endured a smelly egg facial. After the singing of egg-related songs and the reading of *eggstatic* poetry, Cook took the plunge wearing a snorkel, mask, and swim trunks—only to hop out about a minute later before he was overpowered by rotten yolks. For a bracing finish, firefighters hosed Cook off. Although his stunts are tied to schoolwide reading goals, the principal and his faculty use them as the basis for math and science lessons as well. For instance, students studied birds and totaled up how many eggs it would take to cover the reclining administrator. Even though Cook lost a set of clothes over that stunt ("I had no idea eggs stained like that," he says), the principal calls the experience rewarding. "It's a lot of fun," Cook says. "I think it humanizes us. People are willing to talk about the stunt even if they feel a little intimidated talking about academics. Parents get involved."

SOURCE: Telephone interview with Alan Cook, August 27, 2002.

No. 37: Got Milk?

Silliness Rating: 5
Gross-Out Rating: 2
Mix-and-Match Possibilities: Stunts Nos. 13, 39, 42

Basic Stunt: Milk a cow at a special school assembly

FRILLS, CHILLS, & SPILLS

- Challenge the district superintendent or another principal to a milking contest.
- As an alternative, milk a goat instead.

LEARNING LINKS

- Make this stunt the culmination of a yearlong "down on the farm" theme. Ask students to use the milk pail to practice figuring volume. Introduce nutrition facts with milk-related activities.

OBSTACLE AVOIDANCE

- Hold a few practice sessions at the dairy providing the cow. Make sure she's calm enough around crowds to refrain from kicking you during the big event.

SUCCESS SNAPSHOTS

- Two cows were better than one at Greensboro, North Carolina's John Van Lindley Elementary when Principal Kathryn Lofquist took on Superintendent Jerry Weast in a milking competition after students met an Accelerated Reader goal. It turned out that Lofquist didn't have a chance; Weast grew up on a dairy farm where he often pitched in on the milking. But the principal proved she was a good sport by kissing her cow after losing the contest, the *Greensboro News & Record* reported (Newsom, 1998a).
- After harvesting the benefits of a yearlong "Reading Down on the Farm" theme, students at Dowagiac, Indiana's Lincoln Elementary watched Principal Max Sala try his hand at milking a prize dairy cow. The rookie managed to extract about half a glass of milk, but the children cheered him anyway. They earned the opportunity to see him in *udderly* silly action by exceeding their annual reading goal, the *South Bend Tribune* reported (Havens, 2000).

CURRICULUM RESOURCES

Duffield, K. S. (2003). *Farmer McPeepers and his missing milk cows.* Flagstaff, AZ: Rising Moon Books.

No. 38: Where in the World?

Silliness Rating: 3
Gross-Out Rating: 1
Mix-and-Match Possibilities: Stunts Nos. 10, 49

Basic Stunt: Challenge students to track you down at school as part of a geography unit

FRILLS, CHILLS, & SPILLS

- After students complete a world geography unit, designate various parts of school as stand-ins for foreign nations. For instance, the cafeteria might be Canada and the playground could be Greece. Have teachers give the children clues as to where in the world you are. Consider pre-taping video hints to your whereabouts. Give prizes to the class that finds you first.
- Consider hosting a geography fair or geography bee on the day of this stunt.

LEARNING LINKS

- This stunt really puts your geography and social studies curriculum on the map, but it can easily be used to boost math and language-arts classes, too.

OBSTACLE AVOIDANCE

- Make sure students have access to up-to-date maps and atlases.

SUCCESS SNAPSHOTS

- Flat Stanley, the title character of a classic book by Jeff Brown, figures prominently in the geography units of many grade schools. Students make Flat Stanley dolls out of paper and mail them to adults who pose them in photos around the world. At Cincinnati, Ohio's Oyler Elementary, students got back more than 600 Flat Stanleys after an ambitious mass mailing. The dolls returned with letters, souvenirs, and even videotapes from interesting people (such as Defense Secretary Donald Rumsfeld and a lady-in-waiting to Queen Elizabeth II) and places (including New York City, Canada, Mexico, Florida, and Idaho). In addition to learning geography lessons, the children honed their letter-writing skills through the project as well. "This is a great thing," one student told the *Cincinnati Enquirer*. "You get to write and get pictures. I like to go places and travel" (Mrozowski, 2003).

- Dahlgren, Virginia's Potomac Elementary scored out-of-this-world bragging rights when one of its Flat Stanley dolls floated onto the International Space Station. After a trip on the shuttle Endeavor, space-man Stanley spent two weeks in orbit, circling the Earth 171 times on a trip that stretched nearly 5 million miles. Stanley made his triumphant return in the company of two astronauts, who discussed their jobs at a special school assembly. The adventure took off with help from the brother of a reading aide, who happens to be a NASA procurement specialist, the Associated Press reported (Dyson, 2002).

CURRICULUM RESOURCES

Brown, J. (1964). *Flat Stanley*. New York: Harper Collins Juvenile.
Handford, M. (1987). *Where's Waldo?* Boston: Little, Brown.
The Learning Company. (2001). *Where in the world is Carmen Sandiego?* Novato, CA: Riverdeep.

No. 39: Cereal Thriller

Silliness Rating: 5
Gross-Out Rating: 2
Mix-and-Match Possibilities: Stunts Nos. 37, 94, 100

Basic Stunt: Jump into a giant bowl of milk while wearing a suit studded with Rice Krispies

FRILLS, CHILLS, & SPILLS

- As part of a series of silly suit stunts, David Letterman had milk poured over him in a giant bowl while dressed in a Rice Krispies-covered outfit in the mid-1980s. It remains one of the most memorable moments from his NBC talk show *Late Night With David Letterman.* If snapping, crackling, and popping don't tickle your fancy, you can always take another page from Dave's book and let small birds peck at you while you wear a suit covered with suet. But I wouldn't recommend that.

LEARNING LINKS

- This stunt lends itself well to a nutrition unit on the importance of eating a healthy breakfast.
- Tie the activity to a service-learning project that collects goods for a local food bank.

OBSTACLE AVOIDANCE

- Use spoiled milk and cereal that's past its expiration date so no one can accuse you of wasting food.

No. 40: Obstacle Coursing

Silliness Rating: 4
Gross-Out Rating: 3
Mix-and-Match Possibilities: Stunts Nos. 86, 94

Basic Stunt: Run the wackiest obstacle course students can dream up

FRILLS, CHILLS, & SPILLS

- Crowd-pleasing obstacles tend to include messy foods, dressing up in crazy costumes, and riding on silly conveyances such as tricycles.

LEARNING LINKS

- Have fun with fitness by focusing a P.E. unit on obstacle-course navigation.

OBSTACLE AVOIDANCE

- You can't avoid obstacles on an obstacle course.

SUCCESS SNAPSHOT

- Inspired by a Nickelodeon show, Principal Sam Shaneyfelt ran an obstacle course dressed as the *"Double Dare* Dude*"* after 520 students at Franklin Township, Pennsylvania's Sloan Elementary read on their own for 2,000 hours. Shaneyfelt's donated tuxedo bit the dust after he bellied over whipped cream and wet sand, slid into a pool of Jell-O, scooped up damp noodles from his knees, and attempted to craft a big bubble by dragging a hula hoop through a vat of soap, water, and corn syrup. "The students are definitely motivated by this process, and they get into reading," the principal told the *Pittsburgh Post-Gazette.* "They start developing a nightly habit of leisure reading. It's not something they've been assigned to do. It's not the drudgery of a homework assignment. It's reading for fun." Shaneyfelt also has hosted a story hour from the school roof dressed as Super Reader, and he has taken a balloon ride decked out in Peter Pan shoes, Corduroy the Bear overalls, and the Cat in the Hat's colorful chapeau (Chute, 1994).

No. 41: Disappearing Act

Silliness Rating: 4
Gross-Out Rating: 1
Mix-and-Match Possibilities: Stunts Nos. 43, 61

Basic Stunt: Enlist a local magician to make you disappear into thin air

FRILLS, CHILLS, & SPILLS

- Learn a few simple magic tricks you can perform for students as a warm-up to your disappearance.

LEARNING LINKS

- With a "Learning Is Magic" theme up your sleeve, you'll soon levitate interest in all areas of the curriculum.

OBSTACLE AVOIDANCE

- Conduct a dress rehearsal or two, just to make sure the magician can make you reappear.

SUCCESS SNAPSHOT

- Decked out in a wizard's hat and robe, Principal Bob Potter disappeared from an assembly celebrating student reading successes at Sugar City, Idaho's Central Elementary. After he appeared to search in vain for the local magician who would assist his departure, the man onstage took off his hat to reveal that Potter had disappeared, leaving the magician in his place. "Hi, I'm Dave Thompson," the mystery man told the students. "I understand I'm here to make Mr. Potter disappear. Anyone seen him lately?" The principal soon reappeared through a paper screen to the accompaniment of the *2001: A Space Odyssey* theme. Potter observed that he was a bit peeved to discover his disappearance received louder applause than his return, the *Idaho Falls Post Register* reported (Davidson, 2002).

CURRICULUM RESOURCES

Lombardo, M. A. (2002). *Mastering math through magic.* Worthington, OH: Linworth.

No. 42: The Big Bucks

Silliness Rating: 5
Gross-Out Rating: 2
Mix-and-Match Possibilities: Stunts Nos. 24, 37, 100

Basic Stunt: Ride a mechanical bull and try to keep from getting bucked off in front of students

FRILLS, CHILLS, & SPILLS

- Dress in your best cowboy duds to put on an exciting Wild West show.

LEARNING LINKS

- This stunt ties in well with a yearlong farming theme.

OBSTACLE AVOIDANCE

- Array tumbling pads around the bull to minimize the risk of injury should you be bucked off.

SUCCESS SNAPSHOT

- Teachers and Principal Nona Burling donned cowpoke duds and rode a mechanical bull at Oklahoma City's Ralph Downes Elementary after students blew past a goal of reading for 250,000 minutes in five weeks. Spurred on by the promise of the stunt, they ended up with 329,000 minutes of reading under their belts, the *Daily Oklahoman* reported ("A rough ride," 2003).

No. 43: Hypnosis Hullabaloo

Silliness Rating: 4
Gross-Out Rating: 1
Mix-and-Match Possibilities: Stunts Nos. 41, 61

Basic Stunt: Bring in a hypnotist to put you into a trance in front of students

FRILLS, CHILLS, & SPILLS

- Don't keep that trance to yourself—enlist other faculty and staff members to take their share of good-natured humiliation onstage.

LEARNING LINKS

- Put on your thinking cap to create a related science unit on the mysteries of the brain.

OBSTACLE AVOIDANCE

- Set firm ground rules that ensure the hypnotist won't use the power of suggestion to venture into suggestive territory.

SUCCESS SNAPSHOT

- Known as "Dr. Soul," hypnotherapist Jim Soules has made a mysterious name for himself conducting hypnosis presentations at Southern California schools. His free programs, delivered to both students and educators, use humor and hypnosis to deliver the basic message, "Don't give up on education." The presentations proved popular, Soules told the *San Diego Union-Tribune*, because "humor intelligently delivered opens people up and lets them relate to you and listen to a message delivered from the heart" (Roberts, 2001).

No. 44: Pie by the Pound

Silliness Rating: 5
Gross-Out Rating: 3
Mix-and-Match Possibilities: Stunts Nos. 32, 62, 86

Basic Stunt: Challenge students to a pie-eating contest

FRILLS, CHILLS, & SPILLS

- Ice cream will work as well—but watch out for those nasty ice-cream headaches.

LEARNING LINKS

- Counterbalance this treat-eating extravaganza with nutrition lessons on making healthy snack choices.

- Launch a *pi*-calculating contest to tie this stunt into your math curriculum.

OBSTACLE AVOIDANCE

- With nut allergies a growing concern in schools, make sure the pies aren't even topped with almond shavings.

SUCCESS SNAPSHOT

- It's not good to attend school on an empty stomach, but students at Evergreen Elementary in Carol Stream, Illinois, tried to work up big appetites when they faced off against Principal Jean Peterson and Assistant Principal Andrea Paterala in a pie-eating contest. The event marked the completion of a service learning project that gathered more than 4,000 items for a food bank. Contestants had to plant their faces in a raspberry pie, find the piece of bubblegum hidden inside, and then blow a bubble. Students won every head-to-messy-head match. In other years, the administrators have raced each other on tricycles, and performed carols on the school roof. The annual stunt "really seems to motivate them," Paterala told the *Chicago Daily Herald* (Greco, 2000).

CURRICULUM RESOURCES

Bokhari, N. (2001). *Piece of pi: Wit-sharpening, brain-bruising, number crunching activities with pi.* Fort Atkinson, WI: Highsmith Press.

No. 45: 'Chute the Works

Silliness Rating: 5
Gross-Out Rating: 1
Mix-and-Match Possibilities: Stunt No. 10

Basic Stunt: Go skydiving to reward sky-high student achievement

FRILLS, CHILLS, & SPILLS

- Try to obtain a parachute and flight suit in school colors.

LEARNING LINKS

- A cross-curricular unit on flight will help your science, social studies, and math programs soar.

OBSTACLE AVOIDANCE

- Follow the safety training sessions closely, and plan a backup stunt in case of bad weather—or cold feet.

SUCCESS SNAPSHOTS

- Principal Madalyn Mincks of Issaquah, Washington's Clark Elementary took a dive for her students after they raised $10,000 for the local PTA. That dive took her 8,000 feet from an airplane to the ground—in the company of a professional skydiver. Mincks's mother chipped in $50, on the condition that her daughter would stay on the ground. But the principal scooped up the check and took the plunge anyway. She didn't think the stunt was that big of a deal. "I love roller coasters, and I'm not scared of heights," Mincks told the *Seattle Times*. Actually, she added "This is a way that I can say, 'I am scared, but I can be courageous'" (Vinh, 1999).
- Principal Sharon Pristash of West Duluth, Minnesota's St. James Catholic School promised to skydive from 10,000 feet if her students raised $10,000 during a community cleanup project. When the children reached the goal, the local newspaper covered the story, which was then picked up on regional radio and by national newspaper reporters. By the time the big day rolled around, Pristash found her feat featured on the syndicated TV show *Inside Edition*. "I can't believe how much attention this has been getting," she told the *Duluth News-Tribune*. "It's hilarious" (Frederick, 2000).

CURRICULUM RESOURCES

Carson, M. K. (2003). *The Wright Brothers for kids: How they invented the airplane—21 activities exploring the science and history of flight*. Chicago: Chicago Review Press.

No. 46: Room-o-Sumo

Silliness Rating: 5
Gross-Out Rating: 1
Mix-and-Match Possibilities: Stunts Nos. 72, 86

Basic Stunt: Wrestle students, faculty, and staff members in giant foam sumo suits

FRILLS, CHILLS, & SPILLS

- Adopt a wacky stage name to wrestle under, and take on a matching personality when you enter the ring.

LEARNING LINKS

- Tie in a social studies unit on Japan and its serious sumo subculture.

OBSTACLE AVOIDANCE

- Even though the suits are padded, place several tumbling mats around the ring to cushion your falls.

SUCCESS SNAPSHOTS

- He may be a recent winner of the serious Milken Family Foundation Educator of the Year Award, but Principal David O'Shields is known around Clinton, South Carolina's Bell Street Middle School as an administrator who will go to silly lengths to inspire students. One year, he pumped students up for an important standardized test by appearing as a sumo wrestler in a prep class called Wildcat Wednesday Fundamentals (WWF). "He wrestled the faculty," Assistant Principal Dennis Dotterer told the *Greenville News*. "He really wanted to motivate the students for the test" (Washington, 2003).
- Principal Thomas Murphy donned a sumo suit and took on teachers at Bally, Pennsylvania's St. Francis Academy after students wrestled their way through more than 4,100 books in a September reading challenge, the *Allentown Morning Call* reported ("Sumo wrestling . . . ," 2003).

- To kick school spirit up a notch, teachers at Lakewood Ranch, Florida's Lakewood Ranch High battled each other in the ring during a Faculty Fight Night event. The mock bouts featured giant boxing gloves and super-sized sumo suits. "I see it as getting the kids to come out and support the teachers that support them all year around, and it gives them a reason to come back to the school at night for a positive thing," organizer Don French told the *Sarasota Herald-Tribune* before squaring off in a marquee match. "And as a kid, when you see your teachers participating in these kinds of events, it makes them more human" (Smith, 2002).

- Their sumo suits were stuffed with foam rubber, but the hearts of Principal Bruce Haddix and Assistant Principal Richard Hollingshead were filled with the desire to motivate students when they squared off at Indianapolis, Indiana's McClelland Elementary. They staged the wild wrestling match to get students pumped up for a round of standardized exams. "With the No Child Left Behind legislation, we're feeling the responsibility to improve test scores more acutely," Haddix told the *Indianapolis Star.* "This is a way to get kids fired up, and encourage them to really focus and do the best job they can." Added Hollingshead, "We want to reward effort. And since we don't have much money, we had to be creative in coming up with ways to do that." The showdown ended in a draw, when the administrators belly bumped each other so hard, they both ended up on their backs on opposite sides of the ring (Cobb, 2002).

No. 47: Puddles of Pudding

Silliness Rating: 5
Gross-Out Rating: 4
Mix-and-Match Possibilities: Stunts Nos. 94, 100

Basic Stunt: Roll around in a pool of pudding

FRILLS, CHILLS, & SPILLS

- Substitute mud or Jell-O if you have an aversion to tapioca.

LEARNING LINKS

- Ask math classes to practice finding volumes by calculating how much pudding will be needed to submerse you completely.

OBSTACLE AVOIDANCE

- Wear goggles to keep goop out of your eyes, and wear clothes you won't mind throwing away.

SUCCESS SNAPSHOTS

- After students at Hughston Elementary in Plano, Texas, read for a combined 150,000 minutes over the course of a month, principal Luanne Collins rewarded them by diving into a 76-gallon vat of chocolate pudding. Wearing snorkel and flippers, she made quite a splash while a local radio station provided live coverage. Gifted Programs Specialist Lisa Baumann suggested the idea, and tied the stunt into many lessons for her fifth-grade class. Related activities focused on subjects ranging from mathematics and letter writing to advertising and promotions. "When principals do these kinds of things, it really shows a commitment to the students and an involvement in their learning," Donna Criswell, executive director of curriculum and instruction for the Plano Independent School District, told the *Dallas Morning News*. "It's something they can give of themselves to the students" (Gillman, 2000).
- Many school administrators grapple with their superintendents over the issues, but Principal Myrna Bengston of Chelsea, Oklahoma's Chelsea Elementary took the concept to the extreme when she wrestled district Superintendent Joe Gill in a tub of green Jell-O on the school playground. The pair mucked around in the "Chelsea" green gelatin after students met a monthlong reading goal at the start of the school year. "It's crazy, I know, but this has been a super incentive for my students to build on a habit of reading," Bengston told the *Daily Oklahoman* (Killackey, 1992).
- A Norwegian teacher found herself immersed in culture of a different kind when her young students poured yogurt all over her on the playground of Oslo, Norway's Lilleaker School. It wasn't a malicious prank. In fact, Hanne Eilhardt Pedersen donned a bikini in preparation for the dousing—which she agreed to after her students made good on a promise to read 70,000 pages. If they'd lost the bet,

Pedersen's students would have had to act out nursery rhymes during an assembly. Instead, they won the day by reading 82,317 pages during the school year. "This is absolutely the craziest thing I'd done during the ten years I've been teaching," the instructor told Oslo's *Aftenposten.* As if we needed more proof that America exports its popular culture to the world, Pedersen got the idea after reading about a U.S. teacher who took a jelly bath when his students hit a reading goal (McNamara, 2001).

- A year after buzzing over the school in a biplane to reward students for reaching a reading goal, Principal Pam Truxillo of St. Bernard, Louisiana's St. Mark Catholic School kept her feet on the ground. Actually, her feet—along with the rest of her body—were submerged in a pool of green Jell-O while the school's top 11 readers sprayed her with whipped cream. The girl who read the most books topped Truxillo off with a papier-mâché cherry. "It gets kids motivated to read, and the more they read, the better they get at it," the principal told the *New Orleans Times-Picayune* (Cannizaro, 2000).

- The mud was flying when Principal Kathy Poloni lowered herself into a wading pool full of goop to reward the 500 students at Sacramento, California's Trajan Elementary for reading 1.7 million pages over the course of the school year. Spurred on by the promise of the stunt, the children regularly exceeded their reading quotas. "Every week, I was amazed to see them read more than they were required to," teacher Ralphene Lee told the *Sacramento Bee* (Hart, 2002).

No. 48: Snake Handling

Silliness Rating: 5
Gross-Out Rating: 4
Mix-and-Match Possibilities: Stunts Nos. 6, 13, 100

Basic Stunt: Wrap yourself in a boa—a boa constrictor, that is

FRILLS, CHILLS, & SPILLS

- If one snake seems too tame, consider climbing into a box slithering with several serpents of varying sizes.
- Really give students an icky thrill by planting a kiss on the snake's head while it's giving you a squirmy hug.

LEARNING LINKS

- Belly up to a natural-science unit focusing on the reptile kingdom.

OBSTACLE AVOIDANCE

- Stay away from all venomous varieties, and deputize a snake wrangler to keep the critters from slithering under the bleachers to freedom.

SUCCESS SNAPSHOT

- Principal Alan Cook wasn't speaking with a forked tongue when he promised students at Orangevale, California's Green Oaks Fundamental Elementary that he'd spend time with a snake if they met their annual reading goal. But he wasn't expecting to be lowered into a glass case filled with squirming serpents. "I was thinking little garter snakes, but they had some gentleman from an exotic pet store bring in 17 snakes, from four-inch corn snakes to a 60-pound python," Cook recalls. "That was a shock. They were quite happy to curl up to a warm body."

SOURCE: Telephone interview with Alan Cook, August 27, 2002.

No. 49: Literary Theft

Silliness Rating: 4
Gross-Out Rating: 1
Mix-and-Match Possibilities: Stunts Nos. 2, 25, 38, 66, 74, 94

Basic Stunt: Portray a favorite character from children's literature

FRILLS, CHILLS, & SPILLS

- Give students the opportunity to vote for which character you'll play on the designated day. Popular choices include Captain Underpants, the Cat in the Hat, Gandalf from the *Lord of the Rings*, Harry Potter, Peter Pan, and Mary Poppins.

LEARNING LINKS

- This is a great stunt to promote reading, and there are so many options available you can choose a fresh character to portray year after year.

OBSTACLE AVOIDANCE

- Pick a character students will easily recognize. Your childhood favorite may be a relative unknown today.

SUCCESS SNAPSHOTS

- Every fall, Principal Fred Nidiffer dresses up as a kid-friendly literary hero and spends a day on the roof of Knoxville, Tennessee's A. L. Lotts Elementary to reward scholastic achievement. After catching cold one year in a Tarzan loincloth, Nidiffer recently donned the flowing robes of Gandalf the wizard. "*Lord of the Rings* has been my favorite book for 40 years, and I finally get to dress up as a character," he told the *Knoxville News-Sentinel* before making his ascent. One other bonus: "I'll be a whole lot warmer." In other years, Nidiffer has hit the roof decked out as Elvis Presley, Barney the Dinosaur, a Swiss mountain climber, and a University of Tennessee football player (McRary, 2002).

- Emulating Sandy Duncan, Principal Nancy R. Allen of Duncan, Oklahoma's Woodrow Wilson Elementary donned the green garb of Peter Pan and took flight after her students met a monthlong reading challenge that kicked off the school year. With the aid of a harness-and-pulley system, Allen flew off the roof straight into a celebration that included a giant ice-cream sundae laid out in a new gutter pipe. "My kids are really excited about this," Allen told the *Daily Oklahoman* just before making her entrance. "This will also show them that principals are human, and they like to play a little, too" (Killackey, 1992).

- Principal Bruce Johnson revealed his shockingly silly alter ego to the students of Stanardsville, Virginia's Nathanael Greene Elementary after they improved their standardized test scores. Johnson appeared on the school's roof as Captain Underpants, hero of the popular children's books series. The outfit included a red cape, white undershirt, and large white underpants worn over his clothes. "We'll have to do this every year to get the scores up," Superintendent Ray Dingledine told the *Daily Progress*. Added Johnson, "They'll laugh at me out here, but when it comes to being in the office, there's no arguing" (Andrews, 2002).

No. 50: Record Breaking

Silliness Rating: 3
Gross-Out Rating: 2
Mix-and-Match Possibilities: Stunts Nos. 28, 86

Basic Stunt: Help set a world record

FRILLS, CHILLS, & SPILLS

- The Guinness record for simultaneous balloon popping stands at a mere 1,603. Basketball fans in Hays, Kansas, set the mark at a college game in early 2004.
- The world's tallest Lego tower scraped the sky at 24.91 meters in 1998. The structure, built in Estonia, consisted of 391,478 plastic bricks.
- The largest omelet on record was cooked up in 1994 by Swatch workers in Japan. The 160,000-egg dish covered 128.5 square meters.
- Getting ready to construct a new school building? The record for most people participating in a groundbreaking ceremony was set at an Oklahoma Goodyear Tire facility in 2002 by 1,038 shovel-wielding employees.
- The largest outdoor pillow fight on record took place in Kansas in 2003. It included 645 feather-covered participants.
- A measly 731 people in Birmingham, England, set the record for most people covered by slime at the same time, when they had 840 liters of yellow goop dumped on their heads in 1999.

LEARNING LINKS

- Choose a world record that dovetails with your most important curricular focus. For instance, you might attempt to construct the world's largest pop-up book to encourage children to read more.

OBSTACLE AVOIDANCE

- Carefully follow the rules for recording your record-setting attempt. Guinness judges have disallowed many otherwise successful attempts due to a lack of proper documentation. For complete guidelines, go to http://www.guinnessworldrecords.com.

SUCCESS SNAPSHOTS

- Shakopee, Minnesota's Sun Path Elementary attempted to set a world record while hewing to a reading theme when students crafted the biggest pop-up book ever made. The giant tome weighed in at 300-plus pounds, stood eight feet tall, and expanded to 14 feet wide when the covers were opened. The six-page book took five months to create. "I'm always trying to teach kids to dream big," art teacher Jane Smith told the *Minneapolis Star Tribune.* "Just because they're young doesn't mean they can't fulfill their dreams." The project was funded by a $1,000 grant and the proceeds from T-shirt and candy sales. A local construction firm donated wooden sheets that became the pages. "I've worked with kids for over 17 years and I've never had kids so excited about art," Smith said. "I can't keep them out of the art room" (Kumar, 2002).
- Math teacher Dan Meyer recently set the world record for stringing together the most paper clips in 24 hours. After recovering from a failed attempt in 2003, Meyer completed his quest on a Saturday in early 2004 at Sacramento, California's Florin High. Fueled by espresso, pizza, bagels, and grapes—and aided by a volunteer who kept pushing new paper clips his way—the teacher completed a mile-long chain with 30 minutes to spare. The feat shattered the old record set by a Swedish man, and seemed destined to enter the *Guinness Book of Records.* "The last four hours, I was not a happy camper," Meyer told the *Sacramento Bee.* "My forefinger and thumb would not work at all." However, he added, "I'm very content right now" (Guinness, 2003; Robertson, 2004).
- Students, teachers, and administrators at seven Ottawa, Canada, schools flopped into the snow to set the world's record for most

snow angels made at the same time in 2003. With 2,282 participants flapping their arms and legs, the schools shattered the previous record of 1,791 snow angels set in North Dakota, the *Ottawa Citizen* reported (Hughes, 2003).

CURRICULUM RESOURCES

Guinness world records 2004. (2003). London: Guinness Media.
Morse, J. C., Terban, M. & Brace, E. (2003). *Scholastic book of world records 2004.* New York: Scholastic Books.

No. 51: Velcro Flight

Silliness Rating: 5
Gross-Out Rating: 1
Mix-and-Match Possibilities: Stunts Nos. 94, 97, 100

Basic Stunt: Launch yourself against a Velcro wall in a Velcro suit

FRILLS, CHILLS, & SPILLS

- Late-night talk show host David Letterman immortalized this stunt during the February 28, 1984, episode of *Late Night With David Letterman* on NBC. You can re-create one of his most memorable moments by leaping from a small trampoline onto the wall, as he did.
- If you're feeling particularly acrobatic, try jumping on the wall backwards, or even upside down.

LEARNING LINKS

- Tie this stunt into a comprehensive science unit on inventions. Inspired by hooked burrs that stuck to his clothes during walks in the Swiss countryside, George de Mestral patented the hook-and-loop fastening tape known as Velcro in 1951. He began his inventing career in the early 1900s, when he patented the design for a toy airplane at the age of 12, but Velcro was de Mestral's biggest triumph. Today his fasteners are used on everything from tennis shoes to NASA spacecraft.

OBSTACLE AVOIDANCE

- Amusement companies rent Velcro walls and jumpsuits for $400-$500 a day, but crafty staffers and parents might be able to help sew you a suit and put together a suitable wall for much less. Hint: Stick the "hook" tape on the wall, and the softer "loop" tape on the suit.
- Place gymnastics pads between your launch point and the wall to break any falls.

SUCCESS SNAPSHOT

- When juniors at Green Cove Springs, Florida's Clay High recorded the highest scores in the county on a standardized test, they were allowed to don Velcro jumpsuits and launch themselves onto a Velcro-covered wall. Principal Pete McCabe then let the football team deposit him fully clothed in a community swimming pool. Later, he plunged off the high dive in his still-soggy suit. "This is all about the kids, rewarding them for their academic excellence," McCabe told the *Florida Times-Union*. "This is a celebration; we are here to have fun." The event also featured a dunk tank and wrestling in foam-rubber sumo suits (Cravey, 2000).

CURRICULUM RESOURCES

Roberts, R. M., & Roberts, J. (1994). *Lucky science: Accidental discoveries from gravity to Velcro, with experiments*. New York: John Wiley.
Wulffson, D. L. (1999). *The kid who invented the Popsicle: And other surprising stories about inventions*. New York: Puffin.

No. 52: Get Dunked

Silliness Rating: 5
Gross-Out Rating: 1
Mix-and-Match Possibilities: Stunts Nos. 8, 29, 49, 67

Basic Stunt: Let students try to dump you into a dunk tank

FRILLS, CHILLS, & SPILLS

- Dress up in a frog suit, Little Mermaid getup, or other aquatic costume to add more fun to the festivities.

LEARNING LINKS

- Ask math students to calculate the volume of water needed to dunk you completely.

OBSTACLE AVOIDANCE

- Consider wearing a wetsuit under your costume to keep the cold at bay.

SUCCESS SNAPSHOTS

- Principal Melvin Steals went down with the ship to keep the reading program afloat at Cranberry Township, Pennsylvania's Haine Elementary. Dressed as a pirate, Steals took several dives in a dunk tank when balls thrown by top reading students found their mark. Librarian Sandy Reidmiller dreamed up the stunt. She constructed a mock pirate ship inside the school library and gave students raffle tickets for each book read. Prizes ranged from book baskets to turns at the dunk-tank throwing line. "My philosophy is that if kids like coming to the library, they'll be motivated for the rest of their lives to read," Reidmiller told the *Pittsburgh Post-Gazette*. She added that the dunking stunt "provides a nice reward for reading, because we can't afford to give each one a prize" (Cueni-Cohen, 2004).
- After promising students at Auburn, New York's Genesee Elementary that he'd take a turn in a dunk tank if they reached a reading goal, Principal Robert Reardon decided to get a jump on his stunt. So every Friday for a month before the big event, Reardon roamed the halls wearing swim fins, green clothing, and a papier-mâché frog's head. As he passed classrooms, he would call out in a throaty voice, "Read-it! Read-it!" He wore the same outfit during the dunking session—with one important twist. "I had a wetsuit underneath, so I was very warm," Reardon told the *Syracuse Post-Standard* (LaRue, 1987).

No. 53: Waiting Around

Silliness Rating: 2
Gross-Out Rating: 1
Mix-and-Match Possibilities: Stunts Nos. 11, 15

Basic Stunt: Wait tables in the school cafeteria

FRILLS, CHILLS, & SPILLS

- Dress up as a 1950s diner waitress or soda jerk.

LEARNING LINKS

- Tie in the stunt with a service-learning project that solicits donations for the local food bank.

OBSTACLE AVOIDANCE

- Enlist plenty of assistants from the faculty and staff to keep the lunch hour moving.

SUCCESS SNAPSHOT

- More than half a dozen of the most respected administrators and instructors in the Mentor, Ohio, school district showed up for work at a local eatery during a Celebrity Server Night fundraiser. The educators chipped in their tips to help pay for field trips and other educational endeavors, the *Cleveland Plain Dealer* reported (Matzelle, 2004).

No. 54: Kid for a Day

Silliness Rating: 4
Gross-Out Rating: 1
Mix-and-Match Possibilities: Stunts Nos. 11, 94

Basic Stunt: Swap places with a student for a day

FRILLS, CHILLS, & SPILLS

- Load the student's schedule with fun ceremonial activities. For instance, arrange for the child to take board members on a building tour as part of his or her administrative duties.

LEARNING LINKS

- Host a career day in conjunction with the stunt, and set up booths where students can try various interesting jobs on for size.

OBSTACLE AVOIDANCE

- Dress like your students, but resist the urge to parody their speech and actions in a way that might prove hurtful.

SUCCESS SNAPSHOT

- Principal Shelley Viramontez traded roles with a sixth grader at Campbell, California's Monroe Middle School for one day after the boy sold more magazine subscriptions than any other student during a fundraising drive. While Viramontez aced one of the student's pre-algebra tests, the boy scored big points with the administrative staff by showing up for duty with a box of donuts. Later, while the boy principal sealed his popularity by adding five minutes to the morning break for students, Viramontez was busy leading the girls to a kickball victory in P.E. class. She said her favorite part of the day was eating lunch with students. "It was encouraging to see how well they treated me, and I told them I hope that this is the way they would treat any new student coming to school here," the principal told the *Campbell Reporter* (Wicks, 2003).

CURRICULUM RESOURCES

Rodgers, M. (2003). *Freaky Friday*. New York: Avon.

No. 55: Dummy Up

Silliness Rating: 4
Gross-Out Rating: 1
Mix-and-Match Possibilities: Stunts Nos. 8, 19, 94

Basic Stunt: Perform a ventriloquism routine for students

FRILLS, CHILLS, & SPILLS

- As an alternative, consider dressing as a ventriloquist's dummy and working up a comedy routine with a fellow educator.

LEARNING LINKS

- Encourage students to make their own dummies or marionettes as an art project, then ask them to put on their own puppet shows.

OBSTACLE AVOIDANCE

- Make sure students sit close enough to view your ventriloquist act properly.

SUCCESS SNAPSHOTS

- In his 17 years as principal of Fair Lawn, New Jersey's Radburn School, James Jones inspired and entertained students by performing his polished ventriloquism act at assemblies. He also gave students a hint about what the spring school play would be by dressing up as a related character every Halloween, the *Bergen County Record* reported. For instance, one year he donned a wig and red dress to indicate that a production of *Annie* was in the offing (Austin, 2003).

- Principal Phil Davis establishes a strong rapport with his students at Greenfield, Indiana's Mount Comfort Elementary with childlike ventriloquist dummies named Jo-Jo and Jody. "You don't have to do puppets," Davis told the *Indianapolis Star*. "But do something that gets the kids' attention and enables you to spend time with them. I recommend an 'MBWA' management style—management by walking around." In addition to toting around the puppets, the principal invites student groups to weekly "Doughnuts With Mr. Davis" breakfast sessions. He also stands at the front door to welcome children as they arrive every morning, regularly dines with them in the cafeteria, extols positive character traits dressed as historic figures such as Johnny Appleseed, and calls each student's parents annually to detail positive contributions their kids have made at school (McCleery, 2003).

CURRICULUM RESOURCES

King, K. (1997). *Ventriloquism made easy.* Mineola, NY: Dover.

No. 56: Check Mates

Silliness Rating: 3
Gross-Out Rating: 1
Mix-and-Match Possibilities: Stunts Nos. 29, 49, 86

Basic Stunt: Participate in a game of human chess

FRILLS, CHILLS, & SPILLS

- Make the human chess match the centerpiece of a medieval fair, complete with court jesters, madrigal singers, Maypole dances, and even a hobbyhorse jousting tourney.
- Some schools play human checkers games in addition to life-size chess matches.

LEARNING LINKS

- Launch an afterschool chess club with this stunt to help students hone their critical-thinking skills.

OBSTACLE AVOIDANCE

- Set up fun postgame activities for human pieces who get knocked off the board right away.

SUCCESS SNAPSHOTS

- Students dressed in black or white as chess pieces squared off on a human chessboard in the cafeteria at Jacksonville, Florida's Paterson Elementary. Principal Fred Fedorowich, who started the school's chess club, marshaled one group of gifted students against a team led by the advisor of another local school's chess club. After the children practiced in several weekly sessions, the life-size match ended in a draw. "I actually got the idea from the medieval festival in Gainesville, although human chess matches have been around since the Middle Ages," teacher Lisa Lowery told the *Florida Times-Union* (Spengler, 2003).
- A human chess game was just one of the draws at the Chess Challenge held by Tallahassee, Florida's Killearn Lakes Elementary. Principal Margaret Fulton opened the festivities by appearing as the Chess Queen in a cape and crown. Soon, every student in the school was taking turns playing chess on regular boards in the cafeteria against local players. Meanwhile, the human chess game took place under a covered walkway, with the life-size pieces dressed in school colors of green and white. "It is just really exciting to see kids sitting out on the sidewalk playing chess," Fulton told the *Tallahassee Democrat*. "It's been an extremely positive learning experience" (Dunn, 2002).

CURRICULUM RESOURCES

Snyder, R. M. (1991). *Chess for juniors: A complete guide for the beginner*. New York: Random House.

No. 57: Get the Point

Silliness Rating: 4
Gross-Out Rating: 3
Mix-and-Match Possibilities: Stunts Nos. 98, 100

Basic Stunt: Recline on a bed of nails

FRILLS, CHILLS, & SPILLS

- Enlist a teacher to hammer a small cinderblock on your chest while you rest on the nail bed.

LEARNING LINKS

- This is an exciting, memorable way to demonstrate basic principles of physics.

OBSTACLE AVOIDANCE

- Because pressure = force/area, it's important to use many nails to form your bed. For instance, one Southern California science teacher crafted his spiky bed by driving more than 1,700 2.5-inch nails into a wooden platform. It's also crucial to make sure the platform is level and that all the nails are driven in an equal distance so the surface is uniform. After all, if a few of the nails poke out above the rest, they might puncture you when you recline on the bed.
- Some educators allow students to smash five-pound cinderblocks on them as they recline on the nail beds, but it's more prudent to enlist a fellow teacher or administrator to swing the hammer.

SUCCESS SNAPSHOT

- AP Physics teacher Barry Riehle draws gasps from students at Anderson Township, Ohio's Turpin High when he instructs them about the distribution of force. That's because his demonstration consists of doffing his shirt, reclining on a bed of nails, and then inviting a pupil to place a piece of plywood over him followed by a 40-pound cinderblock. To top off the stunt, Riehle invites Assistant Principal John Marshall to crush the block with a sharp sledgehammer blow. "The dynamic instruction he uses to engage the kids in the learning process is the heart and soul of why he's successful," Marshall told the *Cincinnati Enquirer* (Kranz, 2004).

No. 58: Treemendous!

Silliness Rating: 5
Gross-Out Rating: 1
Mix-and-Match Possibilities: Stunts Nos. 22, 94

Basic Stunt: Move your office into a tree for the day

FRILLS, CHILLS, & SPILLS

- If the tree proves too tall an order, you can create a similar effect by setting up your desk in the school courtyard or on the front lawn.

LEARNING LINKS

- Branch into a social studies unit on tree-dwelling cultures, and focus a natural science unit on animals that call the treetops home.

OBSTACLE AVOIDANCE

- Make sure you're secured to the tree with a safety rope at all times.

CURRICULUM RESOURCES

Wyss, J. (1989). *Swiss family Robinson.* New York: Grosset & Dunlap.

No. 59: Take a Dive

Silliness Rating: 4
Gross-Out Rating: 1
Mix-and-Match Possibilities: Stunts Nos. 22, 29, 94, 100

Basic Stunt: Jump off the high dive into a swimming pool fully clothed

FRILLS, CHILLS, & SPILLS

- Challenge members of the swim team to a race as a follow-up activity.

LEARNING LINKS

- Base math activities on the stunt, challenging students to calculate your velocity as you fall, and so on.

OBSTACLE AVOIDANCE

- Make sure you've got a spotter on the scene skilled in CPR.

SUCCESS SNAPSHOT

- When juniors at Green Cove Springs, Florida's Clay High recorded the highest scores in the county on a standardized test, Principal Pete McCabe allowed the football team to deposit him fully clothed in a community swimming pool. Later, he plunged off the high dive in his still-soggy suit. "This is all about the kids, rewarding them for their academic excellence," McCabe told the *Florida Times-Union.* "This is a celebration; we are here to have fun" (Cravey, 2000).

No. 60: Climbing the Wall

Silliness Rating: 3
Gross-Out Rating: 1
Mix-and-Match Possibilities: Stunts Nos. 10, 22, 100

Basic Stunt: Scale a climbing wall to reward top-flight student achievements

FRILLS, CHILLS, & SPILLS

- Dress up as the wall-crawling Spider-Man to give the stunt even more theatrical impact.

LEARNING LINKS

- Tailor math activities to climbing-wall dimensions and popular climbing spots around the world. Focus a geography lesson on legendary mountains.

OBSTACLE AVOIDANCE

- Take a few practice runs before the big day, and make sure you're connected to the wall with a safety rope at all times.

SUCCESS SNAPSHOT

- Principal Tim Stewart pulled a really off-the-wall stunt when students at Clinton, Tennessee's South Clinton Elementary met a reading challenge: He dressed up as Spider-Man and rappelled off the school roof. Firefighters and paramedics supervised the spine-tingling effort. "Two words sum it up: I survived," Stewart told the *Knoxville News-Sentinel.* "I'm willing to do most anything to motivate these youngsters to read good, quality literature" ("Spiderman rappels . . . ," 1995).

No. 61: Split Personality

Silliness Rating: 5
Gross-Out Rating: 4
Mix-and-Match Possibilities: Stunts Nos. 41, 43, 100

Basic Stunt: Enlist a magician to saw you in half

FRILLS, CHILLS, & SPILLS

- Invite the media to cover the year's most shocking school cut. Use the opportunity to make the case for more educational funding.
- Magicians carefully guard their secrets, but the inventor of the first sawing illusion, Horace Goldin, patented the method and device he used in 1923. You can obtain the relevant diagrams and descriptions by requesting Patent No. 1,458,575 from the U.S. Patent and Trademark Office. For ordering information, visit http://www.uspto.gov.

LEARNING LINKS

- Adopt a "Learning Is Magic" theme and even class cut-ups will get in on the act.

OBSTACLE AVOIDANCE

- Very young students might have trouble understanding that the trick is not real. This stunt is probably best reserved for older grade-schoolers.

SUCCESS SNAPSHOT

- To celebrate the power of the written word, Principal Joan Marley of Brookfield, Wisconsin's Hillside Elementary went under a power saw for students after they read for a combined 367,256 minutes in just one month for the "Reading Is Magic" initiative. But Marley emerged from the experience unscathed: A professional magician did the sawing during a special assembly. "I held my breath and crossed my fingers," the principal told the *Milwaukee Journal Sentinel*. "I didn't know if I was going to have to be in some little container." After performing the spectacular stunt, magician Glen Gerard made his own reading pitch to students, telling them, "If you'd like a really cool rope trick or a card trick, go to the library and get a book and read about it" (Clawson, 1996).

No. 62: Bake-Off!

Silliness Rating: 2
Gross-Out Rating: 1
Mix-and-Match Possibilities: Stunt No. 44

Basic Stunt: Participate in a faculty and staff bake-off with student judges

FRILLS, CHILLS, & SPILLS

- Put the frosting on the big day by popping out of a cake.

LEARNING LINKS

- Require contestants to use only natural, healthy ingredients so you can roll the bake-off into a nutrition unit.

OBSTACLE AVOIDANCE

- Consider banning nuts and other ingredients known to cause allergic reactions.

CURRICULUM RESOURCES

Pillsbury Co. (2004). *Pillsbury Best of the Bake-Off cookbook: Recipes from America's favorite cooking contest*. New York: Clarkson Potter.

No. 63: Pigskin Classic

Silliness Rating: 5
Gross-Out Rating: 3
Mix-and-Match Possibilities: Stunts Nos. 8, 13, 100

Basic Stunt: Chase down and attempt to catch a greased pig

FRILLS, CHILLS, & SPILLS

- Give yourself an added challenge by chasing after the porker with one hand tied behind your back.

LEARNING LINKS

- Your barnyard antics could serve as a fitting climax to a yearlong farm theme.

OBSTACLE AVOIDANCE

- Release the pig into a closed-off area so he can't squeal into traffic.

SUCCESS SNAPSHOT

- After students at Hillsboro, Oregon's Evergreen Middle School raised $25,000 for a new Quest Tech computer lab, Principal Lauri Lewis took off after a greased pig. As if that wasn't a wacky enough stunt, she gave the porker a smooch after she finally caught him, the *Oregonian* reported (Maves, 2000).

No. 64: Monkey Business

Silliness Rating: 5
Gross-Out Rating: 1
Mix-and-Match Possibilities: Stunts Nos. 29, 94

Basic Stunt: Bring in a monkey to do your job for a day

FRILLS, CHILLS, & SPILLS

- Visit various classrooms dressed like an old-fashioned organ grinder with your monkey replacement in tow.
- Pass out bananas as you make your rounds.

LEARNING LINKS

- Focus a natural-science unit on our closest mammal cousins.

OBSTACLE AVOIDANCE

- Keep the monkey's handler close at hand throughout the day to keep your substitute on the right track.

CURRICULUM RESOURCES

Rey, M. (1989). *Curious George goes to school.* New York: Houghton Mifflin.

No. 65: Rock On!

Silliness Rating: 3
Gross-Out Rating: 1
Mix-and-Match Possibilities: Stunts Nos. 16, 17, 88

Basic Stunt: Perform in a faculty-staff rock band

FRILLS, CHILLS, & SPILLS

- Dress the part, wearing sequins and a long "hair metal" wig, for instance.

LEARNING LINKS

- Ask the music teacher to enlist and train a group of backup singers.

OBSTACLE AVOIDANCE

- Avoid student injuries by banning all mosh-pit action.

SUCCESS SNAPSHOT

- After a school-year's worth of practicing, Margaret Fulton, principal of Florida's Killearn Lakes Elementary, joined several faculty and staff members in a rock band performance to celebrate the student body's accumulation of 60,000 Accelerated Reader points. Fulton also gave herself a punky green hairdo for the show. As kids hit various milestones along the way, the principal performed such mini-stunts as getting her ears pierced for the first time. "I just want to motivate them to read beyond their expectations," Fulton told the *Tallahassee Democrat*. "I want to provide to them an extra incentive and to give them practice in setting goals and following through" (Dunn, 2003).

No. 66: Reading Marathon

Silliness Rating: 3
Gross-Out Rating: 1
Mix-and-Match Possibilities: Stunts Nos. 2, 9, 25, 49, 71, 83

Basic Stunt: Read stories aloud for an entire school day

FRILLS, CHILLS, & SPILLS

- Tell the kids you'll read until you're blue in the face. At the end of the day, take a break and return done up in blue makeup.

LEARNING LINKS

- In addition to promoting reading, the stunt can be the culmination of a service-learning project that raises money for a good cause.

OBSTACLE AVOIDANCE

- Stock up on water and throat lozenges to help maintain your voice and keep you comfortable. Take at least a five-minute break every hour.

SUCCESS SNAPSHOTS

- Principal Rob Jakubowski talked until he was nearly blue in the face one day at Hartford, Connecticut's Jefferson School. But he wasn't chastising the grade-schoolers in his charge; rather, he was treating them to an all-day Reading Marathon. His feat took him to all of the school's 22 classrooms, where he pulled favorite stories from a backpack that also contained water, throat lozenges, and stuffed animals based on children's-book characters. The principal's stunt rewarded students for reading 3,000 books in just one month. "We're trying to show kids that reading is not just a subject in school," Jakubowski told the *Hartford Courant*. "It's fun" (Chuang, 2000).
- Teens at Buena Park, California's Buena Park High recently held a 72-hour reading marathon, far outpacing an earlier world record 53-hour event conducted by Italian students. They cracked the books in the school auditorium as part of teacher Ron Carcich's annual "Read Around the Clock" challenge to his remedial students, who read anywhere from three to seven years below grade level. "If you go to most schools, reading is for nerds and for geeks," one junior told the *L.A. Times*. "But for us at this school, people want to be a part of it." Fellow instructor Jim Foreman set up a Web feed of the event so parents could check in on their children. "I'm just doing my part to support this tremendous feat," Foreman said. "This is a prime example of what's right with education" (Yoshino, 2004).

No. 67: All Wet

Silliness Rating: 5
Gross-Out Rating: 2
Mix-and-Match Possibilities: Stunts Nos. 52, 85, 100

Basic Stunt: Subject yourself to a barrage of water balloons

FRILLS, CHILLS, & SPILLS

- Bring in the big firepower for your defense by inviting representatives of the fire department to come in and hose the children down.

LEARNING LINKS

- Use water balloons to teach a unit on velocity and other physics principles.

OBSTACLE AVOIDANCE

- Under-fill small balloons with water to minimize both the mess and the sting they'll cause.

SUCCESS SNAPSHOTS

- Every year, Principal Bruce Short raises the reading goal for students at Monroeville, Pennsylvania's University Park Elementary. And at the end of each year, he rewards the children with increasingly memorable stunts. Once, he faced his fear of heights by taking flight in a hot-air balloon. He also has kissed a duck and been pelted with wet sponges. "The more they read, the better they are, and it keeps them away from the TV," Short told the *Pittsburgh Post-Gazette*. "What amazes me is . . . when you see children getting off the bus, they're carrying library books. When sitting in the rooms, they pull a book out of their desks, and they're reading. At lunchtime and recess, the kids have their books with them" (Chute, 1994).
- When students at Chappaqua, New York's Roaring Brook Elementary met a "Fired Up About Reading" challenge, Principal Mark Soss rewarded them by inviting local firefighters to hose him down at school, the *Westchester County Journal News* reported (Gorman, 2002).

No. 68: Just One Hitch

Silliness Rating: 1
Gross-Out Rating: 1
Mix-and-Match Possibilities: This stunt stands on its own.

Basic Stunt: Get married at school

FRILLS, CHILLS, & SPILLS

- If you're already married, consider renewing your vows in front of students.

LEARNING LINKS

- Focus a social studies unit on wedding ceremonies of cultures around the world.

OBSTACLE AVOIDANCE

- Make sure your significant other is ready to take this big leap in front of so many tiny strangers.

SUCCESS SNAPSHOT

- Students at Seattle's Madrona K-8 who wanted to attend Principal Rickie Malone's wedding had to crack the books every evening for three months. The elementary pupils had to read for 20 minutes a night, while the middle-schoolers were asked to log a full half-hour. After enjoying many interesting stories, nearly 360 qualifying children were further rewarded for their efforts with front-row seats to Malone's Valentine's Day nuptials. School literacy coach Jan Toth floated the idea as soon as she found out the principal had gotten engaged. Malone, who has been an educator for more than three decades, quickly warmed to the concept. The ceremony, held at the school, featured the choir's rendition of "Chapel of Love," as well as original poetry readings by several students. The principal hoped the stunt would help students become lifelong readers. "Three months is enough to start a habit," Malone told the *Seattle Times* (Shaw, 2004).

No. 69: Bound for Success

Silliness Rating: 4
Gross-Out Rating: 1
Mix-and-Match Possibilities: Stunts Nos. 22, 94

Basic Stunt: Let students tie you to a cafeteria chair during lunch hour

FRILLS, CHILLS, & SPILLS

- Impress students and staff alike by breaking free of your bonds with an escape artist's trick or two.

LEARNING LINKS

- Study the life and times of Harry Houdini as part of a social studies unit.

OBSTACLE AVOIDANCE

- Make sure a trusted deputy will be on the scene to break you free at the end of the hour—or if trouble should arise.

SUCCESS SNAPSHOT

- A Pennsylvania elementary principal was fit to be tied when students met their reading goal under a "Bound for Literacy" initiative, so she allowed herself to be roped to a cafeteria chair. "Just before lunch, several PTA mothers armed with a bundle of jump ropes bound me securely, taped my mouth and hoisted me into a chair on a raised platform in the cafeteria," the principal recounted to Dear Abby. "Then the children filed in. Of course, they giggled and waved—but to my astonishment, the kids in both sessions were so quiet you could hear a spoon drop. I was amazed! One of the older children later told me, 'We didn't want to take advantage of you while you were all tied up'" (Van Buren, 1999).

CURRICULUM RESOURCES

Burleigh, R. (2002). *The secret of the great Houdini.* New York: Atheneum.
Sutherland, T. T. (2002). *Who was Harry Houdini?* New York: Grosset & Dunlap.

No. 70: Stage Fright

Silliness Rating: 2
Gross-Out Rating: 1
Mix-and-Match Possibilities: Stunt No. 29

Basic Stunt: Play a cameo role in the school play

FRILLS, CHILLS, & SPILLS

- Give students several silly options for your walk-on part, and then let them select which one you'll play in a schoolwide vote.

LEARNING LINKS

- This stunt inherently draws focus to the drama curriculum, but it also can tie in to a language-arts project on reading and writing plays.

OBSTACLE AVOIDANCE

- Wait for the inevitable hooting and hollering to die down before delivering your lines so your grand performance isn't lost in the crowd reaction.

No. 71: Balancing the Books

Silliness Rating: 3
Gross-Out Rating: 1
Mix-and-Match Possibilities: Stunts Nos. 2, 25, 49, 66, 86

Basic Stunt: Compete in a book-balancing contest

FRILLS, CHILLS, & SPILLS

- Challenge students and faculty members to walk a short obstacle course while balancing stacks of books on their heads and in their hands. Award book trophies to the school's record-setting text balancers.
- Tie in a schoolwide reading goal with the theme "Reading on My Mind."

LEARNING LINKS

- Focus P.E. activities on helping students improve their balance.
- Create a consumer math unit focusing on financial book balancing to prepare students for their first checking and savings accounts.

OBSTACLE AVOIDANCE

- While adults might be able to handle hardcovers, ask students to balance paperbacks so their toes don't get squished when the book towers inevitably collapse.

CURRICULUM RESOURCES

Dropo, Dr. (1998). *How to do balancing tricks and stunts.* Colorado Springs, CO: Piccadilly Books.

No. 72: Step Into the Ring

Silliness Rating: 5
Gross-Out Rating: 2
Mix-and-Match Possibilities: Stunts Nos. 46, 94

Basic Stunt: Participate in a mock pro-wrestling match

FRILLS, CHILLS, & SPILLS

- Pro wrestlers have been known to hit each other with folding chairs and other props when the referee isn't looking, causing fake blood to flow. Consider attacking your opponents with oversized classroom materials such as inflatable pencils instead.
- Adopt a stage name that pokes fun at your reputation around the school or the subject you teach. Maybe you're The Disciplinarian, The Math Marauder, or even The Shusher.

LEARNING LINKS

- Focus a P.E. unit on traditional wrestling moves.
- Encourage children to develop their critical thinking skills with discussions about the relative reality of professional wrestling bouts.

OBSTACLE AVOIDANCE

- Place several tumbling mats around the ring. After all, even stunt falls cause real impacts.

CURRICULUM RESOURCES

Albano, L. (2000). *The complete idiot's guide to pro wrestling.* New York: Alpha Books.
Mazer, S. (1998). *Professional wrestling: Sport and spectacle.* Jackson: University Press of Mississippi.

No. 73: A Real Goal Getter

Silliness Rating: 2
Gross-Out Rating: 1
Mix-and-Match Possibilities: Stunts Nos. 7, 86

Basic Stunt: Play soccer or floor hockey goalie and give every child a free shot from the penalty line

FRILLS, CHILLS, & SPILLS

- In the days leading up to the event, walk the halls bouncing a soccer ball—or toting a hockey stick and wearing a goalie mask.

LEARNING LINKS

- Tie this stunt into a P.E. unit on soccer or hockey, and ask students to use professional sports statistics in math activities.

OBSTACLE AVOIDANCE

- Stretch well and strap on as many pads as possible before running the goalie gauntlet.

No. 74: Seuss for Breakfast

Silliness Rating: 4
Gross-Out Rating: 3
Mix-and-Match Possibilities: Stunts Nos. 2, 49, 66, 71, 94

Basic Stunt: Serve students a breakfast of green eggs and ham

FRILLS, CHILLS, & SPILLS

- If you're going to do this stunt, go all the way and dress up like the Cat in the Hat or some other memorable Dr. Seuss character.
- Serve a side of peaches in honor of *James and the Giant Peach.*

LEARNING LINKS

- Tie this stunt into a fitness unit on the importance of eating a balanced breakfast.
- Use the occasion to promote participation in your school's breakfast program.

OBSTACLE AVOIDANCE

- Remember: A little food coloring goes a long way.

SUCCESS SNAPSHOTS

- After the 400 students at Tishomingo, Oklahoma's Tishomingo Elementary fed their minds with 1,000 books in the first month of school, Principal Gary L. Webb fed their tummies by serving up a breakfast of green eggs and ham in the cafeteria. Dressed as the Cat in the Hat, Webb spent the rest of the day popping into classrooms for brief reading sessions. "I wanted to do something strange but educationally significant," Webb told the *Daily Oklahoman* (Killackey, 1992).
- During the recent "Seusscentennial" celebrating the 100th birthday of Theodor Geisel—a.k.a. Dr. Seuss—Principal Carolyn Green dressed in a striped top hat á la the *Cat in the Hat* and served green eggs and ham to the book-hungry students of Thousand Palms, California's Della S. Lindley Elementary. "I want to inspire the excitement of reading," Green told the *Desert Sun* as she applied white face paint and black whiskers (Woo, 2004).

CURRICULUM RESOURCES

Seuss, Dr. (1960). *Green eggs and ham.* New York: Random House.

No. 75: A Change in the Weather

Silliness Rating: 2
Gross-Out Rating: 1
Mix-and-Match Possibilities: Stunt No. 21

Basic Stunt: Fill in for a local TV weatherman

FRILLS, CHILLS, & SPILLS

- As students near the schoolwide learning goal, mark their progress on a giant weather map. Change the icon from a cloudy sky to a sunny day by the time they're done.

LEARNING LINKS

- This stunt will dovetail nicely with a science unit on weather.

OBSTACLE AVOIDANCE

- Don't wear blue on camera unless you want to appear as a disembodied head when you stand in front of the chroma-key screen.

SUCCESS SNAPSHOT

- Principal Bob Ziegler stepped in for the local TV weatherman to deliver a forecast after students at New Hope, Minnesota's New Hope Elementary met a reading goal. His silly stunts have led to significant circulation increases at the school library. "We've heard from kids and parents saying that had it not been for that reading contest, they wouldn't be reading as much as they are now," Ziegler told the *L.A. Times*. "It is hokey and it doesn't work for everybody. But it works for some" (Bryant, 1994).

CURRICULUM RESOURCES

Breen, M., & Friestad, K. (2000). *The kids' book of weather forecasting: Build a weather station, read the sky & make predictions!* Charlotte, VT: Williamson Publishing.

No. 76: Bubbly Performance

Silliness Rating: 5
Gross-Out Rating: 2
Mix-and-Match Possibilities: Stunts Nos. 97, 98

Basic Stunt: Step into a tank of water while wearing an Alka-Seltzer suit

FRILLS, CHILLS, & SPILLS

- On September 6, 1984, talk-show host David Letterman delighted *Late Night* viewers by slipping into a suit encrusted with Alka-Seltzer tablets and lowering himself into a giant bowl of water. The resulting explosion of fizz created a hilarious do-it-yourself jet-tub effect that fans remember fondly to this day. If you want to follow further in Letterman's comedic footsteps, consider re-creating some of his other suit stunts. For one, he stepped into a giant vat of yogurt with pockets full of tortilla chips. For another, he was lowered into a tank of water while wearing a suit covered with sponges. He also dressed in a suit studded with marshmallows, which he tried to roast with a torch. That stunt, although amusing, failed.

LEARNING LINKS

- Tie this stunt into a fun unit focusing on silly science experiments.

OBSTACLE AVOIDANCE

- When Letterman performed this stunt, he did so wearing goggles and an air tank—and for good reason. When writer Steve O'Donnell tested the Alka-Seltzer suit in the 3,785-liter water tank constructed for the show, he was so overcome by fizzy carbon-dioxide fumes that he briefly blacked out.

No. 77: Rube the Day

Silliness Rating: 4
Gross-Out Rating: 1
Mix-and-Match Possibilities: Stunts Nos. 86, 98

Basic Stunt: Challenge students to build a giant Rube Goldberg device that does something wacky to you

FRILLS, CHILLS, & SPILLS

- Make this stunt part of a schoolwide invention fair honoring Rube Goldberg, the Pulitzer Prize-winning satirical cartoonist who specialized in sketching out complex machinery designed to complete simple tasks.

LEARNING LINKS

- This stunt ties in well with units on science and engineering. After all, *Webster's New World Dictionary* defines a Rube Goldberg device as "any very complicated invention, machine, scheme, etc., laboriously contrived to perform a seemingly simple operation."

OBSTACLE AVOIDANCE

- Thoroughly test the machine for safety before you submit to being raised into the air or otherwise manhandled by it.

SUCCESS SNAPSHOT

- Camped at the business end of an amazing Rube Goldberg device, Acting Principal Scott Aston found himself lifted two feet off the ground in a chair attached to a rope as confetti fell and sirens blared during an assembly at North Canton, Ohio's Clearmount School. The device, dubbed "The Magnificent Motion Machine," was part of an outreach program developed by a local science museum. Students were charged with starting the machine by creating "a

Rube Goldberg machine that moves energy along a path in the most creative, complicated and noisy way possible," the museum's educational outreach coordinator told the *Akron Beacon Journal*. One class took the "noisy" part to heart, filling a kettle with marbles that swung like a pendulum to start the device. They adorned the pot with wind chimes "purely for added noise," teacher Susan Farinacci noted with pride (Galloway, 1997).

CURRICULUM RESOURCES

Wolfe, M. F. (2000). *Rube Goldberg: Inventions!* New York: Simon & Schuster.

No. 78: Three-Wheelin'

Silliness Rating: 4
Gross-Out Rating: 1
Mix-and-Match Possibilities: Stunts Nos. 8, 86, 94

Basic Stunt: Participate in a tricycle race

FRILLS, CHILLS, & SPILLS

- If you're really adventurous, consider learning some unicycle tricks instead.

LEARNING LINKS

- Gear up for a social studies unit on the history of cycling.
- Create a freewheeling fitness unit with a cycling theme.

OBSTACLE AVOIDANCE

- Set a good example for students by strapping on a bicycle helmet for your wacky ride.

SUCCESS SNAPSHOT

- After students at Wesley Chapel, Florida's Quail Hollow Elementary exceeded their annual book-reading goal by nearly 10 percent, Assistant Principal Freda Malphurs toddled around the school all day on a tricycle. In addition to a bicycle helmet covered with paper hands that flapped in the breeze, the administrator also sported giant sunglasses and rubber gloves encrusted with plastic insects. Only a half-hour into her stunt, Malphurs told the *Tampa Tribune,* "It's an exhausting day already." Still, she kept the pedals flying until she had visited every classroom (Blair, 1999).

No. 79: Construction Fun

Silliness Rating: 3
Gross-Out Rating: 1
Mix-and-Match Possibilities: Stunts Nos. 22, 27

Basic Stunt: Spend the day high above your school in a construction cherry picker

FRILLS, CHILLS, & SPILLS

- Reaching for the sky in a cherry picker is a great way to cap off a school construction project—and to draw community attention to the expansion or remodeling effort.

LEARNING LINKS

- Focus math units on construction activities.

OBSTACLE AVOIDANCE

- Keep a guide rope tied to you and the equipment at all times. If the wind picks up, consider cutting the stunt short.

SUCCESS SNAPSHOT

- Facing down his fear of heights, Principal Alan Cook of Orangevale, California's Green Oaks Fundamental Elementary spent a day looking down at his school from the top of a fully extended cherry picker when students met a reading goal. "We were going through construction here at the school, so we tried to tie the stunt into a construction theme," Cook explains. "We had the contractor bring in a 60-foot cherry picker that I sat in all day. I had a cell phone and the kids and I had bullhorns, so I could be out there watching yard duty from a great height. And the kids would call up on the cell phone with questions and suggestions for things to do. The secretary had a bucket so they could raise and lower work for me to do." And he never took a break? "They were going to give me a restroom break, but going up and down was the worst part, so I just stayed up there all day," Cook says.

SOURCE: Telephone interview with Alan Cook, August 27, 2002.

No. 80: Bee Bearded

Silliness Rating: 5
Gross-Out Rating: 4
Mix-and-Match Possibilities: Stunts Nos. 97, 100

Basic Stunt: Wear a beard of bees

FRILLS, CHILLS, & SPILLS

- If the idea of bees on your face is too frightening, consider wearing them on your arm instead. Still scared? Take a break and fix yourself a nice peanut butter and honey sandwich.
- Another option: Help the beekeeper create a bee beard on his or her face instead of offering up your own mug. After all, the process does entail holding the queen in a special cage under your chin—or even inside your mouth. (At least you won't have to worry about the bees carrying you away. It would take nearly 2.4 million honeybees to hoist a 180-pound person, estimates the Puget Sound Beekeepers Association in Washington state.)

LEARNING LINKS

- Create a natural science buzz with a unit on bees.
- Tie this stunt into a spelling or geography bee.

OBSTACLE AVOIDANCE

- Build your buzzing beard in an enclosed area so the bees can't escape and swarm toward students.
- Do not attempt this stunt if you're allergic to bee stings, as it's common to get stung a few times in the process of creating a bee beard.

SUCCESS SNAPSHOT

- Jerry Shaw retired as a teacher and coach at Mishawaka, Indiana's Mishawaka High to devote himself full time to beekeeping—and to amazing students and adults alike by regularly wearing a beard full of buzzing bees. In addition to coaxing three pounds of live bees onto his own chin, Scott has helped form bee beards on brave volunteers such as former National Honey Princess Regina Jager of Iowa. But before he attaches a caged queen to a volunteer's face and smears on some queen-bee pheromone, he makes sure the subject is suitable. "We screen people first by stinging them with a bee, to make sure that they won't have an allergic reaction or panic," Shaw told the *South Bend Tribune*. "You need to see first how they will react to the sting." Clearly, this stunt is not for the skittish. In fact, it's one of the two most dangerous activities outlined in this book. (The other one involves grappling with an alligator.) (Dettmer, 2001)

No. 81: Harness Your Energy

Silliness Rating: 4
Gross-Out Rating: 1
Mix-and-Match Possibilities: Stunts Nos. 24, 29

Basic Stunt: Pull children around the school grounds in a horse cart

FRILLS, CHILLS, & SPILLS

- If you don't want to harness up, consider taxiing the children around in a bicycle rickshaw instead.

LEARNING LINKS

- Tie this stunt into a unit on the history of transportation.

OBSTACLE AVOIDANCE

- Stretch and warm up before pulling the cart. Avoid this activity if you have a bad back.

SUCCESS SNAPSHOT

- Not only did Principal Andrea Petro dress up like a cow when students at Popp's Ferry Elementary in Biloxi, Mississippi, met a reading goal, but she then clambered into a mule-drawn cart and took a tour of the school as giggling children enjoyed the spectacle. Assistant Principal Emanuel Killingsworth went along for the wacky ride as well, duded up as Black Bart, the *Biloxi Sun Herald* reported ("Riding for reading," 2002).

No. 82: Bus Road-e-o

Silliness Rating: 3
Gross-Out Rating: 1
Mix-and-Match Possibilities: Stunts Nos. 2, 11

Basic Stunt: Drive a school bus through a parking-lot obstacle course

FRILLS, CHILLS, & SPILLS

- Add excitement with related activities such as seeing how many students can squeeze into a bus, and how many faculty members it takes to pull an empty bus across the parking lot with a tow rope.

LEARNING LINKS

- Tie this stunt into a traffic-safety unit.

OBSTACLE AVOIDANCE

- Keep children well back from the course while the bus is running.

SUCCESS SNAPSHOT

- Top bus drivers who win state "Road-e-o" events each year advance to a national competition where they vie for bragging rights as the nation's transportation champion. The contests, which emphasize safe driving, include written exams, safety inspections, and obstacle course heats. Navigating the tricky courses requires such maneuvers as stopping on a line, parallel parking, traversing railroad crossings, and offloading students.

No. 83: Hang Around, Around the Clock

Silliness Rating: 3
Gross-Out Rating: 1
Mix-and-Match Possibilities: Stunts Nos. 30, 66

Basic Stunt: Spend 24 straight hours at school

FRILLS, CHILLS, & SPILLS

- Perform this stunt as part of an all-night reading marathon.
- Enlist a radio station to do live updates throughout the evening.
- Set up a Webcam at your desk so students can log on and see you burning the midnight oil.

LEARNING LINKS

- Focus a social studies unit on the night shift and everything that gets done overnight—from baking our bread to nursing our sick—to keep society running smoothly. Invite in parents who work the night shift as guest speakers.

OBSTACLE AVOIDANCE

- Schedule this stunt for a Friday so you can catch up on your sleep over the weekend.

No. 84: Dodge City

Silliness Rating: 4
Gross-Out Rating: 1
Mix-and-Match Possibilities: Stunts Nos. 73, 86

Basic Stunt: Compete in an adults versus children dodge ball tournament

FRILLS, CHILLS, & SPILLS

- Even the playing field by allowing the students to compete in larger teams and directing the adults to participate with one hand tied behind their backs.

LEARNING LINKS

- Tie this stunt into a fun-and-games P.E. unit.

OBSTACLE AVOIDANCE

- Use soft rubber balls to keep the pain to a minimum on both sides of the gym.

CURRICULUM RESOURCES

Brailler, J. M. (2002). *Play ball: The world's best ball games.* New York: Price Stern Sloan.

No. 85: Slip 'n' Sliding Away

Silliness Rating: 4
Gross-Out Rating: 2
Mix-and-Match Possibilities: Stunts Nos. 67, 86

Basic Stunt: Launch yourself down a Slip 'n' Slide on the school lawn

FRILLS, CHILLS, & SPILLS

- Dress up in wacky beachcomber garb before making your big splash.
- Hold a water-themed day of fun and games that includes a dunk tank and water-balloon fights.

LEARNING LINKS

- Focus science and fitness units on water-related themes.

OBSTACLE AVOIDANCE

- Be careful not to damage the grass with a combination of heavy foot traffic and too much water.

SUCCESS SNAPSHOT

- Lake Gibson, Florida's Evangel Christian School holds a Beach-a-thon celebration every fall to kick off the school year and celebrate the annual fundraising drive for school improvements. Held at a nearby lake, the party features water-balloon fights and tubing on the water. But the highlight comes when faculty members join students, staffers, and parents in racing down a Slip 'n' Slide. "We all get to work together as a team, raise money, play and get soaking wet," high school English teacher Jennifer Dibble told the *Lakeland Ledger* (DiCesare, 2003).

No. 86: Have a Field Day

Silliness Rating: 3
Gross-Out Rating: 1
Mix-and-Match Possibilities: Stunts Nos. 40, 44, 46, 56, 63, 67, 72, 78, 81

Basic Stunt: Pit the faculty and staff against the students in a schoolwide Olympiad

FRILLS, CHILLS, & SPILLS

- Fun events worth considering: obstacle courses, knee hockey, sack races, three-legged races, egg pushing, relay races, and tug-of-war challenges.

LEARNING LINKS

- Add an academic aspect to the games with a spelling bee, math games, or a general knowledge bowl.

OBSTACLE AVOIDANCE

- Avoid hard feelings by offering separate awards for students and adults.

SUCCESS SNAPSHOTS

- It's teachers versus students at the annual United We Play games that mark the end of each academic year at Stratham, New Hampshire's Stratham Memorial School. For instance, during the popular Shoe Fly competition, children and faculty members kick their shoes off for distance. The winner earns the coveted Golden Shoe award. "Actually, it's an old rotten sneaker that they painted gold," Principal Tom Fosher told the *Exeter News-Letter.* "I don't know who would want to hold it." Other events include a human checkers game, an obstacle course, and crab-walk relay races (Nolan, 2002).
- Charlotte, Michigan's Weymouth Elementary put a literary twist on the school Olympics concept. During the Reading Olympics,

students earned stickers featuring gold, silver, and bronze medals every day they recorded up to 20 minutes of afterschool reading. During the 20-day event, classrooms chose nations to represent and decorated accordingly. Students in the class that racked up the most stickers earned real medals—although they weren't made of gold. "Reading really affects every curricular area," teacher Julie Snowden told the *Lansing State Journal*. "Our daily events allow for that instant gratification for the children" (De La Cruz, 2002).

No. 87: Sleep With the Fishes

Silliness Rating: 5
Gross-Out Rating: 3
Mix-and-Match Possibilities: Stunts Nos. 29, 52, 100

Basic Stunt: Step into a vat filled with live fish

FRILLS, CHILLS, & SPILLS

- Add some eels to the mix to make the stunt really memorable.

LEARNING LINKS

- Tie this stunt into a reading theme by dressing up as a bookworm when you feed yourself to the fish.

OBSTACLE AVOIDANCE

- Wear non-skid water socks to avoid ending up as a big flop.

SUCCESS SNAPSHOT

- Principal Bob Potter is known for completing crazy literary-themed stunts when students at Sugar City, Idaho's Central Elementary exceed their reading goals. But he really took the bait one year when he dressed up as a "bookworm" and let a crane lower his wriggling body into a huge fish tank. Why perform such over-the-top antics? "These kids are reading maniacs," Potter told the *Idaho Falls Post Register*. "It's cool" (Davidson, 2001).

No. 88: School Idol

Silliness Rating: 4
Gross-Out Rating: 1
Mix-and-Match Possibilities: Stunts Nos. 16, 65

Basic Stunt: Hold an *American Idol*-style singing contest

FRILLS, CHILLS, & SPILLS

- Dress the part of the pop star whose works you'll be singing.
- Allow top-achieving students to serve as your snarky panel of judges.

LEARNING LINKS

- Ask the music teacher to help students covertly work up a few hot vocal numbers to show you how it's really done.

OBSTACLE AVOIDANCE

- Warn students that they might want to bring earplugs to your big performance.

SUCCESS SNAPSHOT

- Faculty and staff members at Riverside, California's Norte Vista High pumped up students for a round of standardized tests by putting on a talent-show parody of the Fox TV show *American Idol.* Instead of belting out the tunes themselves, contestants lip-synched songs as they imitated acts ranging from Metallica to Michael Jackson. "It's important for the kids to see us with a sense of humor," psychology teacher Meg Decker told the *Riverside Press-Enterprise.* Added one senior, "It's pretty off the hook—a whole bunch of teachers doing something you didn't expect. It's one of the few times I can actually have a smile at school." At the end of the hour-long event, Principal Ray Johnson briefly addressed the importance of the upcoming exams. "All we ask is for each of you to give your best effort and represent Norte Vista," he told the students (Lou, 2003).

No. 89: Frozen Moments

Silliness Rating: 4
Gross-Out Rating: 1
Mix-and-Match Possibilities: Stunts Nos. 19, 94

Basic Stunt: Spend the day appearing at various places around the school frozen like a statue

FRILLS, CHILLS, & SPILLS

- Heighten the effect with costumes and makeup like those used by *tableaux vivant* performers on the streets of New Orleans and other cities.
- Lead games of freeze tag at recess.

LEARNING LINKS

- Mold an art unit around the study of classic statuary such as Rodin's *The Thinker.*
- Craft drama activities that explore mime and *tableaux vivant* performances.

OBSTACLE AVOIDANCE

- Take regular stretching breaks to keep from tightening up.

No. 90: Hit Parade

Silliness Rating: 4
Gross-Out Rating: 1
Mix-and-Match Possibilities: Stunts Nos. 4, 7, 8, 29, 49

Basic Stunt: Get silly on a parade float

FRILLS, CHILLS, & SPILLS

- Promote your school's accomplishments to the community while showing them your fun side in one of your city's annual parades.

LEARNING LINKS

- Enlist your art classes to design and construct the float, while language-arts classes brainstorm an appropriately wacky theme.

OBSTACLE AVOIDANCE

- Promote school teamwork by inviting other faculty and staff members to join in on the float fun.

No. 91: Gym Dandy

Silliness Rating: 3
Gross-Out Rating: 1
Mix-and-Match Possibilities: Stunts Nos. 35, 94

Basic Stunt: Perform a wild gymnastics routine

FRILLS, CHILLS, & SPILLS

- Show off your prowess on the rings and parallel bars. At the very least, work up a silly rhythmic gymnastics presentation complete with swirling ribbons.

LEARNING LINKS

- Tie this stunt into a P.E. unit on gymnastics.

OBSTACLE AVOIDANCE

- If you don't have any gymnastics training in your background, consider taking a tumble to a different stunt.

CURRICULUM RESOURCES

Hacker, P., Malmberg, E., & Nance, J. (1996). *Gymnastics fun and games: 51 activities for children.* Champaign, IL: Human Kinetics.

No. 92: Later 'Gator

Silliness Rating: 5
Gross-Out Rating: 2
Mix-and-Match Possibilities: Stunt No. 100

Basic Stunt: Wrestle an alligator

FRILLS, CHILLS, & SPILLS

- I don't recommend that you actually wrestle an alligator. That's far too dangerous. But if there's a wild-animal park near your school with an educational outreach program, there is a relatively safe alligator stunt you can pull that will thrill your students to no end. Ask the handler to flip the alligator onto its back. This will cause so much blood to rush to the reptile's tiny brain that it will momentarily pass out. With the handler close by, gently rub the alligator's stomach. This will rouse the beast and cause it to flip back over into a standing position while you beat a hasty retreat. Thus you will have wrestled an alligator. I once had the distinct pleasure of participating in this stunt at Reptile World near Rapid City, South Dakota. Although I was only 12 at the time, the memory sticks with me to this day.

LEARNING LINKS

- Put some teeth into your natural science program with a unit on alligators and other reptiles.

OBSTACLE AVOIDANCE

- Make sure the alligator remains on its leash—and that the leash remains firmly in the hands of the handler—throughout its visit. This is one of the two most dangerous stunts outlined in the book (along with wearing a bee beard), and as such, it should not be attempted by the faint of heart.

No. 93: Punkin' Chunkin'

Silliness Rating: 4
Gross-Out Rating: 2
Mix-and-Match Possibilities: Stunts Nos. 86, 98

Basic Stunt: Participate in a "punkin' chunkin'" contest

FRILLS, CHILLS, & SPILLS

- Look to the World Championship Punkin' Chunkin' event for contest ideas and inspiration. Its online home is http://www .worldchampionshippunkinchunkin.com. Held in early November, when there's still plenty of "ammunition" left over from Halloween, the competition was founded in 1986 by a fun-loving group of friends in Millsboro, Delaware. Recent contests have drawn as many as 25,000 spectators, 80 competitors, and worldwide media coverage.

LEARNING LINKS

- Use punkin' chunkin' contests to introduce basic theories of physics. For instance, catapults work on the principle of resistance, while trebuchets rely on counterweights to propel objects into the sky.

OBSTACLE AVOIDANCE

- Small pumpkins can travel surprisingly long distances when launched from catapults and air cannons. Send them flying far away from windows—and unsuspecting passersby.
- Catapults can malfunction and send their cargo screaming backwards, so keep the direct path clear behind your machines as well.

SUCCESS SNAPSHOTS

- The annual punkin' chunkin' contest at Lakeland, Florida's All Saints Academy requires entrants to build a trebuchet, catapult, slingshot, or onager no taller than six feet and capable of hurling a

7- to 9-pound pumpkin. During the inaugural competition in the fall of 2003, a simple catapult made of wood and bicycle tires won the day when it launched a pumpkin an impressive 46 yards down the school's football field. "The kids really put a lot of work into this project," physics instructor John Smith told the *Lakeland Ledger.* "They all learned that although their device may have been working the day prior to the contest, the slightest change in release point could alter the success of the contraption" (Lay, 2003).

- Thirty meters was the record toss during the first punkin' chunkin' competition at Louisville, Kentucky's Farnsley Middle School. Students employed a catapult to set that initial record in the autumn of 2003. But the contest awarded prizes by category, so there were winners in the air cannon and trebuchet heats as well. "It is just so integral to what we're doing in the eighth grade, as far as the scientific method and looking at how to build something, how to test something, how to make it better," science teacher Christi Hart told the *Louisville Courier-Journal.* Added technology coordinator Debbie Sweitzer, "What we try to do is offer the kids a chance to look at math, science, and technology in a totally different way, and this is about as different as you can get" (Hall, C., 2003).

CURRICULUM RESOURCES

Gurstelle, W. (2004). *The art of the catapult: Build Greek ballistae, Roman onagers, English trebuchets, and more ancient artillery.* Chicago: Chicago Review Press.
Taylor, N. (2000). *America bizarro: A guide to freaky festivals, groovy gatherings, kooky contests, and other strange happenings across the USA.* New York: St. Martin's Griffin.

No. 94: April Foolishness

Silliness Rating: 5
Gross-Out Rating: 3
Mix-and-Match Possibilities: Stunts Nos. 4, 7, 8, 10, 11, 12, 13, 14, 15, 18, 19, 20, 22, 23, 26, 27, 28, 29, 30, 31, 32, 33, 36, 37, 39, 42, 46, 47, 48, 49, 51, 52, 53, 54, 55, 58, 59, 64, 67, 69, 72, 74, 76, 77, 78, 80, 81, 85, 87, 89, 95, 96, 99

Basic Stunt: Get silly on April Fool's Day

FRILLS, CHILLS, & SPILLS

- First thing in the morning, set the clocks ahead to the end of the day. Read the announcements in pig Latin. Have teachers swap classrooms. Serve up oddly colored dishes with even more colorful names in the lunchroom.
- Print up an edition of the school newspaper or newsletter filled with alien sightings and other hoaxes.
- Prank a teacher by calling students to the office one by one until there are no children left in the classroom.
- Need some more ideas for school-friendly pranks? Perhaps these great April Fool's Day hoaxes will give you a mischievous notion or two. In 1998, the Massachusetts Institute of Technology announced it had been sold to the Walt Disney Co., and would be dismantled and moved to the Walt Disney World theme park in Orlando, Florida, where it would add a Scrooge McDuck School of Management. In 1996, *Discover* magazine reported on a new particle. The size of a bowling ball, "the Bigon" supposedly made a brief appearance when a physicist's computer exploded. In 1984, a small Illinois newspaper invited readers to participate in a contest to see who could save the most daylight during the period of daylight savings time. In 1982, a Hong Kong newspaper reported the development of powdered water—just add water and drink. Way back in 1878, a New York City newspaper reported that Thomas Edison had invented a process for converting dirt into food. And the BBC has made a tradition of pulling fantastic April 1 hoaxes on delighted viewers and listeners. For instance, the respected British broadcasting service has reported that the Big Ben clock was going digital, that people with red hair could contract Dutch Elm disease, and that the nation's TV viewers could enjoy their programs in aromatic "Smellovision." But the BBC's most famous hoax concerned a group of Swiss spaghetti farmers. You can view that 1957 "mockumentary" online at http://news.bbc.co.uk/olmedia/70000/video/_70980_aprilfool_vi.ram.

LEARNING LINKS

- By having instructors switch subjects for the day—while teaching real lessons—you'll invigorate both them and their students.
- The week before the big day, promote children's writing and creative-thinking skills by asking them to come up with funny (not mean) pranks they can play on their friends and families.

- Study the history of April Fool's Day, which likely started in 1582 France when King Charles IX introduced the Gregorian calendar and moved the New Year's celebration from April 1 to January 1. Citizens who stuck to the old schedule were mocked. Incidentally, in modern-day France, an April Fool's prank victim is called a *poisson d'avril*, or an "April fish."

OBSTACLE AVOIDANCE

- The older the students are, the more likely it is this stunt will prompt them to attempt some possibly mean-spirited pranks of their own. For that reason, avoid holding an all-school prank day at the high school level.

SUCCESS SNAPSHOTS

- Speech and drama teacher Jim Babcock convinced students at Horton High in Horton, Kansas, that he was taking the semester off and would be replaced by a substitute named Norm De Plume. The next day, April 1, Babcock shaved his long beard and traded his natural fibers for polyester threads and an overflowing pocket protector. He also assumed an officious attitude and authoritarian manner very different from his own laid-back style. Thus camouflaged, the instructor proceeded to fool his students into thinking their worst educational nightmare had come true. When a student threatened to complain to the principal after being berated by Mr. De Plume, Babcock confessed his prank. "He really had everybody fooled," that student told the *Kansas City Star*, calling his teacher "one of the best character actors I've ever seen." Talk about a great drama lesson! (Engle, 1997).
- Pembroke, Massachusetts, teacher Connie Hayes is legendary at North Pembroke Elementary for her perennial April Fool's Day prank. First thing in the morning, she stands on a chair and writes the day's lesson upside down at the top of the chalkboard. When her second-graders ask about it, she simply tells them she wrote out the assignment while standing on the ceiling. Even so, Hayes told the *Boston Globe*, "We teachers always hope April First comes on a weekend because then we can relax. We know that chalk won't be in our erasers" (Hayes, 1999).

CURRICULUM RESOURCES

Brown, M. (1985). *Arthur's April fool*. New York: Little, Brown.

Cobb, V., & Darling, K. (1989) *Bet you can!: Science possibilities to fool you*. New York: Avon.

Cobb, V., & Darling, K. (1983). *Bet you can't!: Science impossibilities to fool you*. New York: Avon.

No. 95: Pole Vaulting

Silliness Rating: 5
Gross-Out Rating: 1
Mix-and-Match Possibilities: Stunts Nos. 7, 27, 29, 94

Basic Stunt: Sit atop a flagpole for the day

FRILLS, CHILLS, & SPILLS

- Preface your stunt with a screening of the 1923 film *Safety Last*, a masterpiece from silent film great Harold Lloyd, known to fans as "The King of Daredevil Comedy." With no special-effects technology available, Lloyd regularly thrilled audiences by performing actual death-defying feats for the camera. In *Safety Last*, he climbs the façade of a building freehand, encountering all manner of obstacles along the way. At one point, pigeons eat nuts off the top of his head; at another, he hangs from the minute hand of a large clock as it tears away from its moorings. During this climb, he makes a dramatic swing from a flagpole that should set up your stunt nicely. Although Lloyd had a safety platform beneath him during most of this famous sequence, he miscalculated the arc of his flagpole swing and exposed himself to a deadly fall. As the actor wrote in the *Boston Post* in 1924, "At the last climb to the highest point, I swing out on a rope from a flagpole, and the pole bends perilously. It did just that and I swung out beyond the platform again, and neither the boys nor I would have been surprised to find myself dropping into space. My luck held." It's a breathtaking moment just the same.

LEARNING LINKS

- Tailor a social studies unit to flags of the world.
- Examine the history of flagpole-sitting contests and other crazes in America's past, from hula-hoops and yo-yos to Beatlemania and pet rocks.

OBSTACLE AVOIDANCE

- Securely tether yourself to the flagpole and abandon your quest at the first sign of lightning or high winds.

SUCCESS SNAPSHOT

- Principal Carl Otten went up a pole when students at Wright City, Missouri's Wright City Elementary vaulted past their at-home reading goals. Otten spent an entire school day atop a mechanical lift tied to the flagpole 15 feet above the entrance. "It's a little out of the ordinary, but it keeps kids hyped up about school," Otten told the *St. Louis Post-Dispatch* as he tried to keep his footing on the tiny platform as the wind kicked up. Added secretary Cathy Heiliger, "Parents think he's really great. He knows how to do things to make the children enjoy school. That's kind of his motto: 'School can be fun'" (Harris, 2002).

No. 96: Eat Your Hat

Silliness Rating: 5
Gross-Out Rating: 1
Mix-and-Match Possibilities: Stunts Nos. 62, 94

Basic Stunt: Eat a baked facsimile of a hat when students attain a difficult academic goal

FRILLS, CHILLS, & SPILLS

- Let students take a crack at a sombrero *piñata* on the big day so they can have their hat and eat it, too—or at least the candy that comes spilling out.

LEARNING LINKS

- Tie the stunt into a "Hat's Off to Reading" theme.

OBSTACLE AVOIDANCE

- This gag will work better on younger students, as older ones might be apt to complain about your kitchen switcheroo.

SUCCESS SNAPSHOT

- Principal Bob Ziegler promised to eat his hat if students at New Hope, Minnesota's New Hope Elementary met an annual reading goal. But on the appointed day, he chowed down on a gingerbread chapeau instead of a cloth cap. Unfortunately, he told the *L.A. Times*, the baked hat tasted worse than a real one would have (Bryant, 1994).

No. 97: Stupid Human Trickery

Silliness Rating: 5
Gross-Out Rating: 2
Mix-and-Match Possibilities: Stunts Nos. 80, 92

Basic Stunt: Participate in a Stupid Human Tricks assembly showcasing the silly hidden talents of teachers, administrators, and even parents

FRILLS, CHILLS, & SPILLS

- Encourage participants to showcase their Stupid Pet Tricks as well.

LEARNING LINKS

- Ask students to poll their families and uncover the hidden talents of their relatives. Challenge the children to imagine themselves as silly superheroes and write stories about how they would use their powers.

OBSTACLE AVOIDANCE

- Make sure teachers and staff members are comfortable showing off their special skills before drafting them into the performance.

SUCCESS SNAPSHOT

- A Stupid Human Tricks assembly of sorts capped off a service-learning project that prompted students at Hillsboro, Oregon's Thomas Middle School to raise nearly $1,500 for a children's hospital. As a reward, administrators and faculty members performed a variety of silly stunts. Principal Mario Alba shaved his hairy legs. Meanwhile, teachers took pies in the face, shaved their heads, twirled batons to disco music, and otherwise treated the students to a foolish good time.

No. 98: Weird Science Fair

Silliness Rating: 5
Gross-Out Rating: 3
Mix-and-Match Possibilities: Stunts Nos. 5, 57, 76, 93

Basic Stunt: Illustrate fascinating scientific phenomena through a series of silly experiments

FRILLS, CHILLS, & SPILLS

- Assume the persona of a mad scientist while performing your experiments.

LEARNING LINKS

- Enlist the assistance of a local science museum's school outreach program to get the most educational bang out of this event. At the very least, check out the Web sites of several of these museums for activity ideas. For instance, San Francisco's Exploratorium offers a splendid online archive of hands-on science lessons at http://www.exploratorium.edu.

OBSTACLE AVOIDANCE

- Place the proper fire extinguishers and other safety equipment close at hand before setting off that first volcanic eruption.

SUCCESS SNAPSHOT

- A local science museum treated students at Carroll, Texas's Carroll Intermediate School to a Weird Science assembly designed to boost their interest in scientific subjects. Wild projects included melting foam packing peanuts with nail-polish remover, and keeping balls afloat with hot air blowers, the *Dallas Morning News* reported ("Fun science," 2001).

CURRICULUM RESOURCES

Downie, N. A. (2001). *Vacuum bazookas, electric rainbow jelly, and 27 other Saturday science projects.* Princeton, NJ: Princeton University Press.

Herbert, D. (1959). *Mr. Wizard's experiments for young scientists.* New York: Doubleday.

Wiese, J. (2004). *Weird science: 40 strange-acting, bizarre-looking, and barely believable activities for kids.* New York: John Wiley.

No. 99: Color Coding

Silliness Rating: 5
Gross-Out Rating: 2
Mix-and-Match Possibilities: Stunts Nos. 8, 94

Basic Stunt: Adopt a color-based theme for the day

FRILLS, CHILLS, & SPILLS

- Whatever color you—or your students—choose for this stunt, let it permeate every aspect of your life for one day. If the color is orange, wear a pumpkin-hued leisure suit, fill your office with orange balloons, don an orange wig, eat Cheddar cheese and oranges for lunch, and so forth.

LEARNING LINKS

- Link your art and science curricula with a project exploring the color spectrum.

OBSTACLE AVOIDANCE

- When selecting a color, remember the adage that there are few tasty blue foods.

SUCCESS SNAPSHOT

- After students at Macon, Georgia's Northside Elementary accumulated more Accelerated Reader points than any other grade school in the county, nine teachers and administrators celebrated by dressing in blue from head to toe. The outfits even included blue fingernails, blue lipstick and blush, and hair spray-painted "neon blue." The hair dyeing took place in front of 900 cheering students at an assembly with "NES is *Blueming* crazy about reading" as its theme. "I think the teachers are enjoying this as much as the kids are," instructional coordinator Diane Swift told the *Macon Telegraph* (Cadette, 2001).

CURRICULUM RESOURCES

Cooper, C. H. (2000). *Color and shape books for all ages.* Lanham, MD: Scarecrow.

No. 100: Fear Factor Assembly

Silliness Rating: 5
Gross-Out Rating: 5
Mix-and-Match Possibilities: Stunts Nos. 1, 6, 13, 26, 28, 36, 37, 47, 48, 52, 57, 59, 60, 80, 87, 92

Basic Stunt: Face your phobias and participate in a series of gross activities

FRILLS, CHILLS, & SPILLS

- Combine several of the yuckiest stunts in the book to create an assembly that will give students fond memories even as it gives you nightmares. Eating bugs, kissing pigs, swimming in slime, and lying on a bed of nails are all fair game for this one.

LEARNING LINKS

- Ask students to discuss and write stories about their biggest phobias and how they might face them.

OBSTACLE AVOIDANCE

- This stunt is not for the faint of heart or the weak of stomach.

SUCCESS SNAPSHOT

- When the 400 students at Orangevale, California's Ottomon Elementary read for a record-setting 519,211 minutes over six months, Principal Janis Stonebreaker happily subjected herself to a promised "Fear Factor" assembly. The local PTA crafted a cringe-inducing series of challenges using dares submitted by kids. First, Stonebreaker reclined in a plastic pool while pet-store employees covered her with boa constrictors and pythons. Next, the principal donned a princess costume and sang "Someday My Prince Will Come" while kissing a frog. Moving to the basketball court,

Stonebreaker attempted five free throws. Every time she missed a shot, gleeful students added an ingredient to a yucky beverage. Before dining on crispy octopus, the administrator gamely sampled the resulting mix of peanut butter, jelly, spinach, vinegar, sardines, and dog food. She capped off the event by fishing a chocolate treat from a pail of mealworms, the *Sacramento Bee* reports. "For the last six weeks, I got to go to your classrooms and see you excited about reading," Stonebreaker told the kids. "So, OK, I had to do some pretty disgusting things, but it was all worth it, and we'll do it again next year in an even bigger challenge" (McGhee, 2003).

CURRICULUM RESOURCES

Butterfield, M. (2001). *Yucky stuff.* Hauppauge, NY: Barron's.
Masoff, J. (2000). *Oh, yuck: The encyclopedia of everything nasty.* New York: Workman.
Monjo, F. N. (2002). *3 kinds of scared.* St. Leonards, Australia: Allen & Unwin.
Waters, R. (2004). *Phobias: Revealed and explained.* Hauppauge, NY: Barron's.

No. 101: Luck of the Draw

Silliness Rating: ?
Gross-Out Rating: ?
Mix-and-Match Possibilities: Any and all stunts

Basic Stunt: Allow students to select the stunt you'll perform if they reach an academic goal

FRILLS, CHILLS, & SPILLS

- Appear at the assembly blindfolded and let top students lead you to your fate.

OBSTACLE AVOIDANCE

- Deputize a trusted colleague to guide the process and gently nudge students away from stunts you'd be unwilling to perform.

SUCCESS SNAPSHOT

- Principal Rick Hunsucker once shaved the letters A and R into his hair when students at Jay, Florida's Chumuckla Elementary met their annual Accelerated Reader goal. But the next year, he decided to inject some mystery into the motivational stunt process. The children all completed writing assignments outlining what crazy situation they wanted to see the principal in if they met the next reading goal. A selection of those suggestions was put to a school-wide vote, with Hunsucker agreeing to complete the winning stunt. How successful have the principal's annual feats proven as a motivational tool? "We have gotten to the place where teachers are having to fuss at kids and say, 'Put your Accelerated Reader book away and complete this assignment,'" he told the *Pensacola News Journal* (Hall, H., 1999).

4 Don't Try This at School

How to Avoid a Stunt Gone Wrong

Because specific stunts present specific challenges, the preceding chapter provides "obstacle avoidance" strategies for all 101 activities. But it's also important to make sure your stunt doesn't run afoul of the following general list of "don'ts" that could derail the big event and even harm your career.

1. Avoid ethnic, racial, and gender stereotypes. If your school mascot uses Native American iconography, for instance, skip the Mascot Mayhem stunt. In the most disastrous recent stunt of this type, an Indiana elementary principal apologized to the community and resigned after appearing in televised morning announcements as an Iraqi official named Niknak-Padiwak Givudogabon, the *South Bend Tribune* reported. The script for the ill-considered performance included a reference to "our beloved Saddam" and the announcement that "you lying Americans will go to a government-sanctioned assembly about bullying and teasing in the gym. Ha! As if you Americans needed lessons in being bullies. Look what you are doing in Iraq" (Maddux, 2003).

2. Don't break a leg. If you're injury-prone, steer clear of physically challenging stunts. As they say, motivational stunts are fun only until someone gets hurt. Brenda Hales, assistant superintendent of a Utah school district, told Salt Lake City's *Deseret News* of a principal who let a student shave his head so closely that his scalp scarred, and another administrator who broke her leg while roller-skating through school dressed as Santa Claus. "The moral to the story is this," Hales said. "Go ahead and do things that are incentives for kids, but make sure no sharp objects or roller skates are involved—or anything else that could cause bodily harm" (Toomer-Clark & Titze, 2000).

3. Take steps to avoid a backlash. Communicate to parents and other members of the school community exactly how your stunt will boost academic achievement. And don't give critics ammunition to accuse you of wasting precious school funds on a frivolous activity (some folks label all fun activities frivolous, even when they lead to concrete educational gains). Pay for your stunt with PTA donations, special grants, or in-kind contributions whenever possible. Speaking of the PTA, getting parent groups involved in the stunt planning process is one of the best ways to insulate yourself from a backlash. A parent-powered steering committee also tends to come up with fun, creative frills—and helps provide the muscle required to successfully pull off a special schoolwide event. If you really want parents to feel like vested owners of the project, decide on two or three stunts you're willing to do, and let them pick which one you'll perform.

4. Draft a backup plan. In case your stunt falls apart at the last minute, keep a plan B activity at the ready. Principal Alan Cook learned that lesson the hard way when one of his stunts at Orangevale, California's Green Oaks Fundamental School was abruptly canceled. "Our theme was 'Reading Is Magic,' and we got a magician who was going to cut me in half and put on a whole show for the kids," Cook recalls. "We had a great time with it all year, but then when he was unloading his magic trick the night before, he dropped the prop and broke it. It came down to, 'We can really cut you in half, or we can disappoint these little children.'" Needless to say, Cook is still in one piece. "That's the year we decided we needed to pretty much be in charge and not depend on anyone else," the principal adds. "And have a contingency plan."

5. Decide what you'll do if students fall short. Once in a while, students won't reach the academic goal that's supposed to trigger the performance of your motivational stunt. Figure out in advance what your response will be if that happens, in consultation with parents and teachers. One option is simply not to perform the stunt. That's the path Alan Cook followed one year when students didn't reach their collective reading goal. "I was supposed to dress up in a Superman suit and do something in the auditorium, but the kids didn't even come close to the goal," the principal recalls. "They missed it by thousands of pages. One thing I do is, I write the students a bulletin every Monday just like I do for the teachers, and we kept saying, 'Here's your goal and here's what you have left to do,' and they didn't do it. Some parents thought I should have done the stunt anyway because the kids tried so hard, but I think it works both ways. If I promise I'll do something, I cannot get out of it. But if they don't meet their end, I don't have to do it. I didn't have any students say, 'That wasn't fair.' The kids were honest about that. It wasn't that they didn't care, but they didn't see that they were unfairly treated."

Another option: Simply go through with the stunt as planned, rewarding effort as some parents at Cook's school suggested. But the most effective solution might be for you to perform a different, slightly less spectacular stunt, and whet students' appetites for a really big show if they succeed in reaching their goal next year.

5 Alert the Media

How to Generate Positive Press for Your Stunt

It might not always seem to be the case, but newspapers and local TV newscasts hunger to tell positive stories about schools in the communities they cover. Unfortunately, simply doing the things you're supposed to be doing—keeping a lid on school crime, delivering steady gains in test scores, and generally turning out class after class of competent students—usually won't grab headlines. But if you can provide reporters with a "hook," or an out-of-the-ordinary context in which to nestle those success stories, you'll soon generate positive press.

Motivational stunts make great story hooks. They couple fun, highly visual events with feel-good stories about extraordinary student achievement—and the dedicated educators who helped them meet their goals. Even so, newsrooms are busy, understaffed places—much like schools—and even great stories often fall through the cracks. Increase the likelihood that your school will earn the positive coverage it deserves by taking the following steps to promote your stunt to the media.

1. Launch an internal media blitz. Start your campaign with the media you produce in-house. Provide regular stunt updates in school newsletters, both in print and online. Create a stunt countdown page on your school Web site. Send information to the district communications office for inclusion in its publications as well. Not only will these stories keep parents and other members of the school community informed about the stunt, they will serve as stealth press releases as well. Beat reporters regularly comb through newsletters produced by the organizations they cover for story tips.

2. Release the information in a timely manner. Don't wait until the day of the stunt to let reporters know about it. And don't send out a press release announcing a spring event when school starts in the fall, either. Properly timing your press outreach will greatly increase your chances of getting the stunt covered. Start by sending out a detailed press release about a week before the big event. Then phone, fax, or e-mail a reminder the day before you perform the stunt. Send the press release home to parents on the same day you mail it to editors and reporters. Doing so will generate additional excitement about the event, remind parents to attend, and alert them to watch for coverage in the local media. Many parents also appreciate receiving a heads-up that the press has been invited to campus.

3. Get personal. Don't address your press release to the generic "editor" at the local paper. Find out which reporter covers your school and send the release directly to that person's attention. When it comes to generating local TV news coverage, find out the name of the station's assignment editor, and address releases to that person. Because motivational stunts provide such fun visual opportunities, you also should address a separate release to the photo editor of the newspaper. You might well get coverage in the form of a section-leading photo with an extended caption that hits the highlights of your students' academic achievements. And more people will read that caption than any story buried inside the paper.

4. Make yourself available. Include as much contact information for yourself as possible in the press release—including an e-mail address along with direct office and cell-phone numbers, if possible. Fairly or not, reporters spike many optional stories when they can't reach sources on the first attempt.

5. The devil's in the details. Make sure each press release includes the time, date, and place of the stunt, as well as information about exactly what the students accomplished to trigger the big event.

SAMPLE PRESS RELEASE

Principal gets silly when students get serious about learning

DATE
For Immediate Release

CONTACT INFORMATION

NAME OF SCHOOL—Principal NAME will perform a silly stunt to celebrate the outstanding academic achievement of students at TIME, DATE, & PLACE. The students DETAILS OF GOAL MET to force PRINCIPAL NAME to live up to a promise of DETAILS OF STUNT.

In addition to motivating students to reach this impressive goal, the stunt has helped bring the school community closer together while energizing the staff and helping the children see their principal's fun, human side.

"PITHY QUOTE," says PRINCIPAL NAME.

References

Chapter 1

Deci, E. L., Ryan, R. M., & Koestner, R. (1999). A meta-analytic review of experiments examining the effects of extrinsic rewards on intrinsic motivation. *Psychological Bulletin, 125*, 627–688.

Fetbrandt, S. (1996, February 5). Some go an extra smile for students. *Riverside Press-Enterprise*, p. B1.

Kohn, A. (1993). *Punished by rewards: The trouble with gold stars, incentive plans, A's, praise, and other bribes.* New York: Houghton Mifflin.

Gillman, L. M. (2000, May 16). Go kiss a pig: Principals and teachers perform crazy stunts to benefit education. *Dallas Morning News*, p. A18.

Jenkins, L. (2000, April 3). For schools, don't bring in the clowning. *San Diego Union-Tribune*, p. B1.

Chapter 2

Coyne, A. L. (2000). *Creating a year-long theme: A teacher's journey.* Columbus, OH: Englefield & Arnold.

Chapter 3

Acosta, M. (2001, June 28). Reading a lot is as easy as pie, Home Gardens students prove. *Riverside Press-Enterprise*, p. B1.

Allegood, J. (1998, May 13). Principals can't worm out of commitment. *Raleigh News & Observer*, p. A1.

Andrews, K. (2002, June 10). Wacky ways to motivate: Educators try to boost scores. *Daily Progress*, p. 1.

Arsenault, M. (2000, January 31). She sets the goal, she pays the price. *Providence Journal-Bulletin*, p. C1.

Austin, C. (2003, July 1). Newly retired principal revels in role as puppet administrator. *Bergen County Record*, p. L2.

Bailey, E. (2002, June 1). Principal faces his fears to fuel student reading. *Los Angeles Times*, p. M2.

Bartholomew, F. (1993, December 1). Kids ketchup on books; principal a hot dog. *Riverside Press-Enterprise*, p. B2.

Benca, J. (2003, January 12). Third-graders get chance to dress up their principal. *Tri-Valley Herald*, p. B1.

Blair, R. (2002, December 21). Children stick up principal. *Tampa Tribune*, p. 1.

Blair, R. (1999, June 9). F-U-N spells last day of Pasco classes. *Tampa Tribune*, p. 1.

Brown, J. A. (2000, January 2). Sleuthsayers solve mystery. *News & Record*, p. 1.

Bryant, R. (1994, May 24). Novel stunts: Many principals resort to silliness to sell students on reading. *Los Angeles Times*, p. M1.

Cadette, S. (2001, May 24). "Blueming crazy": Northside Elementary celebrates reading accomplishments. *Macon Telegraph*, p. 1.

Cannizaro, S. (2000, March 3). Reading kids put principal in Jell-O. *Times-Picayune*, p. B1.

Carter, R. (2002, May 18). "I leave my dignity at the door." *Atlanta Journal-Constitution*, p. E1.

Chipman, I. (2002, May 24). Argos Elementary School principal keeps his promises. *South Bend Tribune*, p. D7.

Chuang, A. (2000, May 1). Principal's marathon of reading rewards students for work. *Hartford Courant*, p. B1.

Chute, E. (1994, June 16). Reading and pupils' "revenge." *Pittsburgh Post-Gazette*, p. E1.

Clawson, L. (1996, February 29). Magic of reading: Principal goes under saw as students reach goal. *Milwaukee Journal Sentinel*, p. 7.

Cleland, G. (2000, July 25). Local news. *Burlington Hawk Eye*, p. 10.

Cobb, N. (2002, September 17). Principals stage a big-time show: Fun-filled sumo match is staged as incentive for students to prepare for testing. *Indianapolis Star*, p. W1.

Cravey, B. R. (2000, August 30). Scholars reap the rewards: Juniors celebrate test results. *Florida Times-Union*, p. M1.

Cueni-Cohen, J. (2004, March 7). Dip into a good book lately? *Pittsburgh Post-Gazette*, p. N7.

Cutrer, C. (2002, April 15). Books rule at school's monthlong jamboree. *Chicago Daily Herald*, p. 1.

Davidson, B. (2002, May 10). Principal delivers on his promise and disappears. *Idaho Falls Post Register*, p. C9.

Davidson, B. (2001, April 26). School welcomes Sir Reads-a-Lot. *Idaho Falls Post Register*, p. A1.

De La Cruz, J. (2002, February 7). Readers prepare for Olympic challenge. *Lansing State Journal*, p. B4.

Dettmer, S. (2001, August 30). "Bearded" beekeeper abuzz with fun at Olde Farmer's Fest. *South Bend Tribune*, p. D7.

DiCesare, B. (2003, September 30). Beach event helps buy computers. *Lakeland Ledger*, p. S3.

Dunn, A. (2002, April 13). Chess a challenge and a game. *Tallahassee Democrat*, p. B1.

Dunn, A. (2003, January 27). An unconventional approach: School principal will sing if students read. *Tallahassee Democrat*, p. 1.

Dyson, C. (2002, December 3). Third-grader's cutout travels with astronauts to space. The Associated Press.

Engle, T. (1997, April 1). Fool's gold: These April 1st pranks are just priceless. *Kansas City Star*, p. E1.

Feber, E. (1999, February 19). Principal goes head over heels to celebrate reading. *Virginian-Pilot*, p. 2.

Fetbrandt, S. (1996, February 5). Some go an extra smile for students. *Riverside Press-Enterprise*, p. B1.

Fine, L. (2000, January 7). But did they all drink their milk? Cow kiss to reward students. *Philadelphia Inquirer*, p. B3.

Frederick, C. (2000, October 18). Principal to sky-dive after students meet pledge goal. *Duluth News-Tribune*, p. B3.

Fun science. (2001, February 4). *Dallas Morning News*, p. S1.

Furgurson, E. B., III. (1999, December 2). How to look like a million bucks: Principal Fader sacrifices hair for his school. *Capital*, p. B5.

Galloway, B. (1997, November 4). Project a real blast: North Canton students devise a dozen methods for triggering machine that levitates a teacher. *Akron Beacon Journal*, p. B1.

Gillman, L. M. (2000, May 16). Go kiss a pig: Principals and teachers perform crazy stunts to benefit education. *Dallas Morning News*, p. A18.

Goldstein, J. (2000, April 28). Reading has a novel (albeit odd) reward. *Raleigh News & Observer*, p. B3.

Goldstein, J. (1997, March 29). To inspire kids, principals will even kiss frogs. *Charlotte Observer*, p. C1.

Gorman, P. (2002, November 28). Bye-bye beard; bye-bye TV. *Journal News*, p. A1.

Greco, C., Jr. (2000, December 18). Principal ends up with pie on her face. *Chicago Daily Herald*, p. 3.

Gregory, M. (1999, May 20). Just clowning around. *Daily Town Talk*, p. A3.

Guinness world records 2004. (2003). London: Guinness Media.

Hall, C. (2003, October 31). Students send pumpkins flying. *Courier-Journal*, p. B2.

Hall, H. (1999, June 4). Principals risk it all for reading. *Pensacola News Journal*, p. E1.

Hanna, R. (2004, March 4). "They just go out and do it" at Schilling Farms Middle. *Memphis Commercial Appeal*, p. CL11.

Harris, D. P. (2002, September 19). Principal hits roof after students meet their summer reading goal. *St. Louis Post-Dispatch*, p. 1.

Hart, M. (2002, June 2). For the love of . . . her students, principal keeps a muddy promise. *Sacramento Bee*, p. N1.

Havens, C. (2000, April 15). Milking reading for all it's worth. *South Bend Tribune*, p. A6.

Hayes, K. (1999, March 28). At school, a free pass to fool around. *Boston Globe*, p. SW1.

Haynes, K. A. (2002, October 26). Students deliver scores for a song: Counselor portrays "Little Mermaid" after school's 66-point spike in Stanford 9 results. *Los Angeles Times*, p. M4.

Hughes, G. (2003, March 8). Snow angels set sights on world record: 2,285 children, teachers, school staff make patterns in the white stuff in aid of fundraiser. *Ottawa Citizen*, p. D3.

Hughes, S. (2000, May 31). Principal takes to the air to encourage students to read. *Shreveport Times*, p. B1.

Hwangbo, K. (1994, April 16). Bookworms: Principal gobbles creepy crawlers to mark read-a-thon's success. *Los Angeles Times*, p. B1.

Jewell, L. (1998, February 13). A kiss is s-s-s-till a kiss, even when you kis-s-s a snake. *Tampa Tribune*, p. 1.

Johnson, J. (2004, February 19). Niles principal is janitor for a day—and vice versa. *Niles Herald-Spectator*, p. 6.

Kelley, A. (2004, March 11). Schools enlist parents as kids' reading partners. *Journal News*, p. A8.

Killackey, J. (1992, September 28). Educators going out on limb: Reading promotions give kids creative push. *Daily Oklahoman*, p. 1.

King, J. J. (2003, March 19). Books bring new worlds to Ellis kids. *Chicago Daily Herald*, p. 3.

Kranz, C. (2004, March 9). Learning physics by doing physics. *Cincinnati Enquirer*, p. C1.

Kumar, K. (2002, April 19). One for the records: Sixth-graders have assembled what may be the world's largest pop-up book. *Star Tribune*, p. B1.

Lay, R. (2003, April 23). Chunkin' punkins: ASA students build catapults and trebuchets for pumpkin hurling contest. *Lakeland Ledger*, p. S2.

LaRue, W. (1987, April 2). School principal takes a bath on student reading bet. *Post-Standard*, p. B1.

Lawson, J. (2003, October 8). Kids cash in on bargains: Hot coupon book sales have Knox principals paying up. *Knoxville News-Sentinel*, p. A1.

Lou, L. (2003, April 2). April foolery turns teachers into idols. *Riverside Press-Enterprise*, p. B1.

Matzelle, C. (2004, February 28). Creative fund-raisers have a serious purpose. *Cleveland Plain Dealer*, p. B1.

Maves, N., Jr. (2000, May 18). Students see a need, raise money for lab. *Oregonian*, p. 16.

Mayes, M. (1999, March 27). Reading has its reward, students find. *Lansing State Journal*, p. B1.

McCleery, B. (2003, February 18). Principal's gift is rapport with kids. *Indianapolis Star*, p. B3.

McGhee, L. (2003, February 27). Fear is not a factor as principal braves stunts: Ottomon students meet their goal for reading and reap the reward. *Sacramento Bee*, p. G1.

McNamara, L. (2001, June 6). Yoghurt flavour teacher keeps her bet. *Aftenposten*, p. L1.

McRary, A. (2002, October 15). Principally, they do stunts at school for the money. *Knoxville News-Sentinel*, p. E3.

Metzler, K. (1992, December 17). Principal scales new heights for literacy. *Washington Times*, p. B4.

Mortensen, K. (2000, March 24). Boise principal shorn of locks to promote reading. *Idaho Statesman*, p. B2.

Mrozowski, J. (2003, May 15). The Stanley Project: Peripatetic paper helps kids learn. *Cincinnati Enquirer*, p. C1.

Mungin, L. (2003, December 5). Students use science to investigate mock murder. *Atlanta Journal-Constitution*, p. JJ1.

Murphy, J. (1997, February 1). Students pile on all the fixings in hot dog stunt. *Lakeland Ledger*, p. F1.

News in brief from the Philadelphia area. (2001, June 7). The Associated Press.

Newsom, J. (1998a, May 26). Holy cow: Milking contest a splash for kids, adults. *News & Record*, p. B1.

Newsom, J. (1998b, May 30). Principals put pride aside. *News & Record*, p. B1.

Nolan, J. (1995, June 2). Kids meet reading challenge; Penrose principal then hits the roof. *Philadelphia Daily News*, p. 41.

Nolan, S. (2002, June 18). Stratham students, teachers end the year as crabby shoe kickers. *Exeter News-Letter*, p. 3.

Perrault, M. (2004, March 1). Palm Desert High School robot wars. *Desert Sun*, p. 1B.

Preston, T. A., & Dinkin, G. (2003). *Amarillo Slim in a world of fat people: The memoirs of the greatest gambler who ever lived.* New York: HarperCollins.

Principal eats crickets to get pupils to read. (2004, March 13). The Associated Press.

Radcliffe, J. (2003, January 23). Principals' stunts turn students to silly putty: Kids will do almost anything to see educators smooch smelly goats or sport spiky pink hair. *Orange County Register*, p. B1.

Ray, V. L. (2003). *School wide book events: How to make them happen.* Westport, CT: Libraries Unlimited.

Reddy, S. (2000, September 4). Let's dance the reading jig. *News & Observer*, p. B1.

Riding for reading. (2002, June 12). *Biloxi Sun Herald*, p. A4.

Roberts, O. (2001, December 31). "You are getting . . . an education." *San Diego Union-Tribune*, p. D1.

Robertson, B. A. (2004, February 18). This time, paper clip chain broke record, teacher says. *Sacramento Bee*, p. B2.

A rough ride. (2003, February 22). *Daily Oklahoman*, p. 1.

Scanlan, D. (2003, May 21). Kids cheer as principal puckers up. *Florida Times-Union*, p. O1.

School celebrates hopping up to an A on FCAT. (2003, August 30). *Palm Beach Post*, p. C1.

Shaw, L. (2004, February 10). Reading becomes students' wedding vow. *Seattle Times*, p. A1.

Shindruk, L. (2002, April 23). Pie throw tops off state science trophy win. *Bellingham Herald*, p. A4.

Siler, R. (2004, March 4). "Running Principals" are making strides. *Los Angeles Daily News*, p. S10.

Smith, K. (2002, October 31). School faculty enters ring for boxing, sumo. *Sarasota Herald-Tribune*, p. H10.

Solomon, L. K. (2003, August 3). Principal duties: Whether it's listening to a parent or yelling into a bullhorn, good leadership has many styles—and is critical to a school's success. *Sun-Sentinel*, p. 1.

Spengler, T. (2003, December 17). Students engage in battle of minds: Human chess game honors retiring principal. *Florida Times-Union*, p. M3.

Spiderman rappels for readers. (1995, March 26). *Knoxville News-Sentinel*, p. AC8.

Sumo wrestling suits him. (2003, May 14). *Morning Call*, p. B1.

Sweeney, N. (2004, February 27). Gifford principal loses hair over school fund-raiser. *Milwaukee Journal Sentinel*, p. B5.

Tan, S. (1998, May 8). Principal loses high-stakes bet with students. *Daily Press*, p. C1.

Tarr, S. (1994, June 1). Principal goes limit for reading program. *Hartford Courant*, p. D6.

Tobin, P. (2004, March 13). Rest from the test; Lake Agassiz school children celebrate the end of a hectic week. *Grand Forks Herald*, p. B1.

Van Buren, A. (1999, March 30). A win-win situation encourages reading. *Chicago Tribune*, p. 7.

Vinh, T. (1999, May 14). The sky's no limit: Principal to make good on fund-raising promise to sky dive. *Seattle Times*, p. B3.

Washington, V. (2003, October 17). Principal wins "Oscar." *Greenville News*, p. B16.

Weaver, A. (2004, February 20). School gets visit by Packer for meeting reading goals. *Manitowoc Herald Times Reporter*, p. A1.

Wicks, A. (2003, October 29). Wacky Wednesday invades the halls of Monroe Middle. *Campbell Reporter*, p. 1.

Woo, M. (2004, March 3). School celebrates Seuss centennial. *Desert Sun*, p. B3.

Yoshino, K. (2004, February 23). For the record, books inspire them; Buena Park students read aloud, aiming for a world mark—and to promote reading. *Los Angeles Times*, p. M4.

Young, L. (1992, May 12). Reading frenzy sends principal through the roof. *Chicago Tribune*, p. D1.

Young, M. (1999, December 9). College Park raised PTA membership roof and put principal on it. *Virginian-Pilot*, P. 3.

Chapter 4

Maddux, S. (2003, April 24). Principal resigns after Iraqi prank. *South Bend Tribune*, p. D3.

Toomer-Clark, J., & Titze, M. (2000, October 1). Educators get bizarre. *Deseret News*, p. B1.

**CORWIN
PRESS**

The Corwin Press logo—a raven striding across an open book—represents the union of courage and learning. Corwin Press is committed to improving education for all learners by publishing books and other professional development resources for those serving the field of K–12 education. By providing practical, hands-on materials, Corwin Press continues to carry out the promise of its motto: **"Helping Educators Do Their Work Better."**